An Anthology
of Contemporary Verse

BLACKIE & SON LIMITED
16/18 William IV Street, Charing Cross, LONDON, W.C.2
17 Stanhope Street, GLASGOW

BLACKIE & SON (INDIA) LIMITED
103/5 Fort Street, BOMBAY

BLACKIE & SON (CANADA) LIMITED
TORONTO

An Anthology of Contemporary Verse

Selected by
Margaret J. O'Donnell, M.A.
*Author of "Feet on the Ground—
An Approach to Modern Verse"*

BLACKIE & SON LIMITED

LONDON AND GLASGOW

First published 1953
Reprinted 1955, 1957

Printed in Great Britain by Blackie & Son, Ltd., Glasgow

CONTENTS

RETURN TO NATURALISM

Poems of comment on the Contemporary Scene   73

ACKNOWLEDGMENTS

The Editor and Publishers make grateful acknowledgment to the following for permission to use copyright poems as stated:

Mr. W. H. Auden and Messrs. Faber & Faber Ltd. for *The Unknown Citizen*, *Musée des Beaux Arts*, and *O What is That Sound* from " Collected Shorter Poems, 1930-1944 " by W. H. Auden; and *Refugee Blues* from " Another Time " by W. H. Auden.

Mr. George Barker and Messrs. Faber & Faber Ltd. for stanzas from *Calamiterror* by George Barker.

Miss Frances Bellerby and Messrs. Peter Davies Ltd. for *The Summer Dove* from " Plash Mill " by Frances Bellerby.

Miss Frances Bellerby for *Genesis* by Frances Bellerby from " The Listener ", 8th September, 1949.

Mr. John Betjeman and Messrs. John Murray (Publishers) Ltd. for *In Westminster Abbey* from " Old Lights for New Chancels " by John Betjeman.

Mr. Edmund Blunden and Messrs. Macmillan & Co. Ltd. for *The Snail*, *The Hedgehog Killed on the Road*, and *After the Bombing* from " After the Bombing and Other Short Poems " by Edmund Blunden.

Mr. Roy Campbell and The Harvill Press Ltd. for *The Birth of Christ* from " Saint John of the Cross ", translated from the Spanish original by Roy Campbell.

Mr. Roy Campbell and Messrs. Faber & Faber Ltd. for *Washing Day* from " Collected Poems " by Roy Campbell, published by Messrs. John Lane, The Bodley Head Ltd.

Mr. Richard Church and Messrs. J. M. Dent & Sons Ltd. for *Reckless* from " Collected Poems " by Richard Church.

Mr. Paul Dehn and Messrs. Hamish Hamilton Ltd. for *Lament for a Sailor* and *Habitué* from " The Day's Alarm " by Paul Dehn.

Mr. Walter de la Mare and Messrs. Faber & Faber Ltd. for *Listen* from " Collected Rhymes and Verses " by Walter de la Mare; and *But, Oh, My Dear, And So to Bed*, and *An Island* from " The Burning Glass and Other Poems " by Walter de la Mare.

Mr. Lawrence Durrell and Messrs. Faber & Faber Ltd. for *On Ithaca Standing* from " A Private Country " by Lawrence Durrell.

Mr. Clifford Dyment and Messrs. J. M. Dent & Sons Ltd. for *Pieta* from " Poems, 1935-48 " by Clifford Dyment.

Mr. T. S. Eliot and Messrs. Faber & Faber Ltd. for stanzas from *The Rock* and for *A Song for Simeon* from " Collected Poems, 1909-1935 " by T. S. Eliot; and *The Dry Salvages* from " Four Quartets " by T. S. Eliot.

Mr. Roy Fuller and Messrs. John Lehmann Ltd. for *The Divided Life Relived* from " Epitaphs and Occasions " by Roy Fuller.

Mr. David Gascoyne and Messrs. John Lehmann Ltd. for *A Tough Generation* from " The Vagrant and Other Poems " by David Gascoyne; also from " The Times Literary Supplement ", 6th October, 1950.

Mr. Kenneth Gee for *Time and the Ocean* by Kenneth Gee from " The Listener " of 27th April, 1950.

Mr. Robert Graves and Messrs. Cassell & Co. Ltd. for *Gulls and Men* and *Saint* from " Collected Poems, 1914-1947 " by Robert Graves.

Mr. G. Rostrevor Hamilton and the Cambridge University Press for *The Way Home* from " Death in April and Other Poems " by G. Rostrevor Hamilton.

Mr. G. Rostrevor Hamilton and Messrs. William Heinemann Ltd. for *The Flaking Pineapple* from " The Sober War " by G. Rostrevor Hamilton.

Mr. Seán Jennett and Messrs. Faber & Faber Ltd. for *Café au Lait* and *Christ's Cross Grows Wings* from " Always Adam " by Seán Jennett.

Mr. Francis King and Messrs. Longmans Green & Co. Ltd. for *The Martyr* from " Rod of Incantation " by Francis King; also from " The Listener ", 1st June, 1950.

Mr. James Kirkup and the Grey Walls Press Ltd. for stanzas from *The Drowned Sailor* by James Kirkup.

Mr. Laurie Lee and Messrs. John Lehmann Ltd. for *Bird* and *Christmas Landscape* from " The Bloom of Candles " by Laurie Lee.

Professor C. Day Lewis and Messrs. Jonathan Cape Ltd. for *The Stand-To, Will It Be So Again?* and *Word Over All* from " Word Over All: Poems " by C. Day Lewis.

The Executors of the late Miss Lilian Bowes Lyon and Messrs. Jonathan Cape Ltd. for *Northumbrian Farm* and *Stone Pity* from " Collected Poems " by Lilian Bowes Lyon.

Mr. Louis MacNeice and Messrs. Faber & Faber Ltd. for *Prayer Before Birth*, *Flight of the Heart*, and *Spring Voices* from " Collected Poems, 1925-1948 " by Louis MacNeice.

Dr. John Masefield, O.M., The Society of Authors, and Messrs. William Heinemann Ltd. for *Delight in Water* from " Wonderings " from " Poems " by John Masefield, and *February Night* from " A Letter from Pontus and Other Verse " by John Masefield.

Miss Averil Morley and The Oxford University Press for *Lapwings in March* and *The Baby* from " The House in the Forest and Other Poems " by Averil Morley.

Mr. Edwin Muir and Messrs. Faber & Faber Ltd. for *Suburban Dream* from " The Voyage and Other Poems " by Edwin Muir; and *The Child Dying* from " The Labyrinth " by Edwin Muir, and from " The Listener ", 26th June, 1947.

Mr. Norman Nicholson and Messrs. Faber & Faber Ltd. for *Bombing Practice* and *Cleator Moor* from " Five Rivers " by Norman Nicholson, and for *The Tame Hare* from " Rock Face " by Norman Nicholson.

Mr. Norman Nicholson for *The Undiscovered Planet* by Norman Nicholson from ". The Wind and the Rain ", edited by Neville Playbrooke, Vol. VI, No. 2, 1949.

Mr. Herbert Palmer and Messrs. George Harrap & Co. Ltd. for *A Fable* from " A Sword in the Desert " by Herbert Palmer.

Miss Ruth Pitter and The Cressett Press Ltd. for *Thanksgiving for a Fair Summer* and *Fair is the Water* from " A Trophy of Arms " by Ruth Pitter.

Mr. William Plomer and the Hogarth Press Ltd. for *September Evening*, 1938, from " Selected Poems " by William Plomer.

Mr. John Pudney and Messrs. John Lane The Bodley Head Ltd. for *So I Praise These* from " Dispersal Point and Other Air Poems " by John Pudney.

Miss Kathleen Raine and Editions Poetry London Ltd. for *Prayer*, *The Rose*, and *Ecce Homo* from " Living in Time " by Kathleen Raine.

Mr. Herbert Read and Messrs. Faber & Faber Ltd. for *Summer Rain* from " Collected Poems " by Herbert Read.

Mr. Henry Reed for *Movement of Bodies* by Henry Reed from " The Listener ", 6th April, 1950.

Miss Anne Ridler and Messrs. Faber & Faber Ltd. for *For This Time* from " The Nine Bright Shiners " by Anne Ridler.

Mr. W. R. Rodgers and Messrs. Martin Secker & Warburg Ltd. for *Autumn Day* from " Awake! and Other Poems " by W. R. Rodgers.

Mr. Alan Ross and Messrs. John Lehmann Ltd. for *Guidebooks* from " Time Was Away: A Notebook in Corsica " by Alan Ross and J. Minton; also from " The Listener ", 20th November, 1947.

Mr. A. L. Rowse and Messrs. Faber & Faber Ltd. for *Cornish Landscape* from " Poems of Deliverance " by A. L. Rowse.

Mr. Siegfried Sassoon and Messrs. Faber & Faber Ltd. for *The Case for Miners, At the Cenotaph, A Flower Has Opened,* and *Since Thought is Life* from " Collected Poems " by Siegfried Sassoon.

Miss E. J. Scovell for *A Blue Day* from " The Listener ", 19th January, 1950.
Miss E. J. Scovell and Messrs. Routledge & Kegan Paul Ltd. for *The Giraffe* from " The Midsummer Meadow and Other Poems " by E. J. Scovell.

Dr. Edith Sitwell and Messrs. Macmillan & Co. Ltd. for *Still Falls the Rain* and *Dirge for the New Sunrise* from " The Canticle of the Rose " by Edith Sitwell.
Dr. Edith Sitwell and Messrs. John Lehmann Ltd. for stanzas from *The Shadow of Cain* by Edith Sitwell.

Mr. Stanley Snaith for *Hiroshima* from " The Listener ", 29th September, 1949, and from " The Common Festival " by Stanley Snaith (Fore Publications).

Mr. Stephen Spender and Messrs. Faber & Faber Ltd. for *To Poets, Airman,* and *The Air Raid Across the Bay* from " Ruins and Visions " by Stephen Spender.

Mr. Hal Summers for *Homage to Thor Heyerdahl* from " The Listener ", 20th April, 1950, and *Prologue to a Theatrical Season* from " The Listener ", 27th July, 1950.

Mr. Dylan Thomas and Messrs. J. M. Dent & Sons Ltd. for *Dawn Raid* and *To Others Than You* from " Deaths and Entrances ", and *Fern Hill* from " Collected Poems, 1934-52 " by Dylan Thomas.

Mr. Terence Tiller and The Hogarth Press Ltd. for *Beggar* and *Camels* from " Unarm, Eros " by Terence Tiller.
Mr. Terence Tiller for *The Fool in " Lear "* from " The Listener ", 23rd January, 1947.

Mr. Ruthven Todd and Messrs. William MacLellan Ltd. for *These Are Facts* and *It Was Easier* from " The Acreage of the Heart " edited by Maurice Lindsay (Poetry Scotland Series).

Mr. Henry Treece and Messrs. Faber & Faber Ltd. for *A Thief to His Lord* and *Lyric* from " The Black Seasons " by Henry Treece.

Mr. Rex Warner and Messrs. John Lane The Bodley Head Ltd. for *Long-tailed Tit* and *Poem* from " Poems and Contradictions " by Rex Warner.

Mr. Vernon Watkins and Messrs. Faber & Faber Ltd. for *Ophelia* from " The Lady with the Unicorn " by Vernon Watkins.
Mr. Vernon Watkins for *Wind and Rain* by Vernon Watkins from " The Listener ", 17th November, 1949.

The Duchess of Wellington and Messrs. Williams & Norgate Ltd. for *Docks, Back to the House,* and *The Traffic Problem in East Anglia* from " Selected Poems " by Dorothy Wellesley.

Mr. Laurence Whistler and Messrs. William Heinemann Ltd. for *Flight* from " The World's Room " by Laurence Whistler.

Miss Margaret Willy and Messrs. Chaterson Ltd. for *Good Friday in War* from " The Invisible Sun " by Margaret Willy.

Mr. Andrew Young and Messrs. Jonathan Cape Ltd. for *Field-Glasses* and *The Shepherd's Hut* from " The Collected Poems of Andrew Young ".

To my godchildren

Sheila

John

Hilary

FOREWORD FOR THE STUDENT

I

Twentieth-century poetry has reached middle age, as have most of the acknowledged poets who are writing to-day. Revolutionary movements have died down, and a calm has set in; but opinions differ as to whether this calm is a sign that out of the throes of experiment poetry has emerged refreshed, renewed, and ready to proceed to a new phase of its development, or whether it has failed to establish any new growth and is falling back on tradition. Nevertheless, one hopes that its emergence into simplicity of form, language, and theme reflects a returning clearness and singleness of vision. In the midst of the terrifying complexities and uncertainties of life to-day, one simple truth stands out in the work of many poets: that the only hope for mankind is in a spiritual rebirth.

We, at this mid-point of the twentieth century, are in sight of the end of that period that began with the Renaissance, that " glorious rebirth " which has, in fact, led us near to destruction. The Renaissance led to the establishment of Humanism, by which man was elevated to a position of supreme importance— man as an individual, equipped with a brain and a will and a skill which made all things possible to him. Man, and no longer God, was the centre of the universe. The increase in learning, discovery, and invention, and

particularly the astonishing advance of scientific knowledge, have led to the glorification of Man, without
regard to his Creator. And this cult of Man has made
possible Nazism and Atheistic Communism at the two
extremes, and the pagan materialism which is destroying our country to-day.

What has all this to do with poetry? Just this: the
many trends in twentieth-century poetry in England
result directly from the age we live in, and to understand the poetry, we must try to understand the age.
Beginning with 1900, we pass through the confident
and prosperous Edwardian and early Georgian years,
when poetry reflected the comfort and leisure and often
gracious living of that time. The poetry sometimes
seems trivial to us now, and a little smug, but we must
not blame the Edwardians and Georgians who, wrapped
in an illusory security, did not foresee the catastrophes
which were to come upon the world. In fact, we may
envy them their sweet untroubled song.

The year 1914 transformed the world. In this
country, once the first glow of patriotic fervour had
faded, people and poets were filled with a horror and
disgust at the waste and futility of war. Then came
the disillusion of the post-war years when the promised
brave new world did not materialize, and the returning soldier was faced with want and unemployment.
Poetry reflected the ensuing mood of cynicism, bitter
hatred, and despair.

Now the poet who retained his belief in God
searched for the cause of this evil, and found it in
himself. He, like T. S. Eliot, whose poems *The Waste
Land* and *The Hollow Men* epitomized the loss of faith
and all spiritual values, sought also the cure in himself:

Shall I at least set my lands in order?

The poet with little or no belief in the spirit, the poet as humanist, saw the evil only in terms of man's physical and material welfare. His anger and concern for the unhappy plight of his fellow-man roused in him a deep pity; and the poet became a crusader against social and political evils and injustice: he became a propagandist for his own political beliefs.

Now it is good to feel pity for others and to strive for the betterment of man's lot; but notice the difference between a poet like Eliot and one like Auden. The one blames himself as sharing the responsibility for evil and sees the salvation of the world in the spiritual regeneration of mankind; and he begins the cure with himself. The other puts the blame on the politicians, the industrialists, the unnamed sinister " They "; and he looks for a solution in the amelioration of man's lot on earth in material welfare and physical freedom.

The Second World War of 1939, as well as plunging humanity still further into peril and misery, proved that man can triumph over both; and the miraculous resurgence of the human spirit that we saw in our own country brought new hope for the future of the world. The spirit of our people triumphed over disaster and danger from bomb and fire, over want and discomfort, over loss and dereliction. The war, with its countless deeds of unimaginable heroism and endurance performed not by supermen but by the common man and woman, proved that men are more than flesh and blood. The war brought confirmation of the divine spirit in man.

This renewed faith we see reflected in much of the poetry written during and since the war. Once grant that man is partly divine, and the solution is simple. Man has worshipped science for the material comforts it has given him, and now science has brought him close to extinction. The scientist is not without blame. Science itself is simply the outcome of man's urge to explore and analyse, to calculate and experiment, but, in explaining the nature of the universe, science has seemed to explain away God. Now the scientist can explain only the material, physical world; he can tell us what elements compose it; but he cannot guide us in our search for the good and the beautiful. Nor can he do more than theorize on the origin of matter. He is therefore seriously at fault when he speaks to a less-informed community as if he were in possession of the whole truth. Modern times have seen the worship of man change to worship of the scientist, and he, arrogant or indifferent in his necessarily narrow field, has thought so much about science and so little about man, that he must accept some responsibility for the unhappy state of the world at the moment.

Modern times have seen also the worship of in-dividual man change to worship of the State, thus investing it with a potentiality for tyranny which has over and over again placed the world in jeopardy. We see to-day the result of Man's shaping his own destiny. Dare we say, then, that those poets who show a growing awareness of a need for religion and belief in God are taking poetry into a decline? Make your own decision. The poems are here to speak for them-selves and for the poets who wrote them. They range from the hard realism and satire of the years between the wars, through the deep humanity of the war years, to a new simplicity and lyricism, and an awareness of beauty once more.

II

In reading the poems reproduced in this anthology, look for evidence of two distinct trends: the atheistic humanist and the Christian—the concern with man and his material state on the one hand, and realization of man's spiritual needs on the other. Cutting vertically through all other classifications is this fundamental difference.

To classify the poems horizontally, some knowledge is needed of the main trends and influences which have been apparent during the first fifty years of the twentieth century.

Before the patriotic fervour of the first months of the 1914-18 war had given place to a clear vision of the grim reality of war, poetry (Georgian poetry) was characterized by conventional subjects, placidity of mood, and a smooth perfection of rhythm suggestive of quiet Sunday afternoons in a drowsy backwater. Growing up at the same time, however, was a very small movement which was to shatter the peace. The Imagists (the name was coined by Ezra Pound), in reaction against Georgian romanticism, decided that poetry was moribund, and that the only hope was to make a new beginning. So, as tradition, they held, had led only to the backwater, all tradition must be discarded. In revolt against sentimental discursiveness they claimed that poetry must be concrete and exact; it must deal with objects; each word must convey one clear image, with no ambiguity. The expression must be concise and exact: it was poetry of the object and the word. Pruned down to essentials in this way, it followed that a poem must be short.

The revolutionaries did not stop here, however, but abandoned all regular pattern. Metre and rhythm went overboard with metaphor and all stylistic devices, and Free Verse came into existence. Here is an Imagist poem by Herbert Read:

Pasturelands

We scurry over the pastures
    chasing the windstrewn oak-leaves.

We kiss
the fresh petals of cowslips and primroses.

We discover frog-spawn in the wet ditch.

(From *Eclogues*, 1914-18.)

This poem, short though it is, illustrates another feature of the Imagists' work, and one which is found in many modern poems: that is, the elimination of connecting links, and a resultant series of unrelated statements and items. Every word means just what it says. The expression is hard, concrete, and angular. There is no comment, no emotion, no evocation. The logical development of this style is seen in the colloquial realism and understatement of many satirical poets like Siegfried Sassoon, W. H. Auden, and Louis MacNeice.

The Imagist movement was finished by the end of the First World War, but its effects persisted. Free Verse, on account of its lack of form and rules, exercised severe discipline upon its serious exponents, but on the other hand it tempted many spurious poets on account of its apparent freedom from restraint. It did, however, make a positive contribution to English poetry by accustoming the ear to the musical possibilities of ordinary speech. Free Verse itself is gone, but it has shaken rhythm out of its careless ease and revived the freedom and vigour which has always marked the verse of our great poets. Most of those who are writing verse to-day have returned to a basis of traditional metre, but with this difference: the lines are not intended to be scanned, but to be spoken with attention to speech rhythm. Rhyme has also returned to favour, but its use is not now determined only by the pattern of the verse: rhyme is used when it suits the poet's purpose, for emphasis and effect; the rhymes appear to be inevitable and not pressed into service; and they need not be perfectly consonant, but may be half-rhymes or merely have a faint echo of similarity. Listen for example to this stanza from Edwin Muir's *Suburban Dream*:

> Wálking the súburbs in the áfternóon
> In súmmer when the ídle dóors stand ópen
> And the áir flóws through the róoms
> Fánning the cúrtain héms

This basic rhythm of 4 and 3 stresses underlies the whole poem, giving regular pattern in speech rhythm, not metre. As for rhyme, there is nothing but the faintest of echoes: "afternoon" and "rooms", "rooms" and "hems". Look for the influence of the Imagists in poems where the rhythm is speech rhythm, where words are used with great exactness and literalness, and where there is little or no attempt to explore the effects of the *sound* of words.

This influence is seen in the poems written by the poets of the First World War and after—poems which deal with the contemporary world of industry and scientific achievement, of commercial and political

rivalries, of war and injustice and human problems.
It is seen in the use of colloquial, unemotional speech,
in which poets like Siegfried Sassoon, Robert Graves,
and Wilfred Owen began the new tradition of satire
which later, in the 1930's, had its chief exponents in
Auden, MacNeice, C. Day Lewis, and Stephen Spender.

These four poets used all their considerable vigour
of intellect and language to attack social and political
conditions. They were Left Wing in their outlook, and
the Abyssinian War and the Spanish Civil War gave
them any amount of inspiration and ammunition for
their denunciation of capitalist governments and middle-
class hypocrisy. Their weapon was satire, their medium
energetic, colloquial words. They were young, in-
telligent, witty, and merciless in their reporting and
comment.

A combination of topicality, racy diction, wit, and
vigour, and the whole revolutionary set-up, made their
poetry attractive to the ordinary man; it was fresh and
new; it had a kick in it. They, and in particular Auden,
did what most poets since Shakespeare have failed to
do: they made ordinary men and women aware of
them. They brought poetry close to the life of Tom,
Dick, and Harry, and made their names familiar to the
man in the street.

This kind of poetry has fanned out in many direc-
tions. Contemporary light colloquial verse stems from
it, and so does the direct naturalistic poetry inspired
by the poet's environment whether it be the country
or the industrial town. Greatest of all, T. S. Eliot
has gone his own way, developing the cult of the word,
from his early colloquial satire, through his exploration
of the Waste Land, always searching for the truth and
the words to express the truth.

That is one stream, which developed logically from the Imagist insistence on reality and hard exactness of expression. Another stream has its source in a recoil from Imagism into Symbolism. The essence of Symbolism is that a word must on no account have one hard fixed image attached to it, but instead, it must convey by its allusiveness, its associations, its evocative power, not so much meaning as feeling and suggestion. An image, yes, but much more in addition. Thus the language of the Symbolists is not direct—it is indirect, suggestive and subtle; it grows and spreads its meaning in the receptive imagination. It gives rise to " Imagery " instead of " images ". There is this difference between the two words: an image can be seen clearly and sharply, but " imagery " is a whole background or rather a hinterland of sensation widening out in a reversed perspective behind the words which call it into being; it is the view through the magic casements opening on the foam of perilous seas in faery lands forlorn.

To understand a poet's symbolism, one must have a receptive and a creative imagination, plus a knowledge of the poet's private language of symbols. The latter one may acquire by assiduous reading of much of the poet's work, a process in which one absorbs his idiom and becomes familiar, by repetition, with his symbols. But, without such a wide acquaintance with other poems, it is obvious that the average reader will find symbolic poetry extremely difficult, if not incomprehensible. Only an explanatory note (preferably by the poet) can lay the poem open to him. On the other hand, much symbolic poetry is pure sensation, which can often be felt even when the meaning is not fully grasped; the poem may be understood intuitively. This is true of much of the work of T. S. Eliot. There

is a thrill, half of beauty, half of fear, and wholly independent of meaning, in these lines:

> Garlic and sapphires in the mud
> Clot the bedded axle-tree.

The Waste Land is full of symbolism which can be felt
without being understood:

> A woman drew her long black hair out tight
> And fiddled whisper music on those strings
> And bats with baby faces in the violet light
> Whistled, and beat their wings
> And crawled head downward down a blackened wall

Symbolism, Allegory, and Metaphor are no new
features of poetry, but with the rise and fall of fashion
they disappear and reappear from time to time. Twentieth-century Symbolism received much of its impetus
from contemporary French poetry, from which came
also another influence—Surrealism.

The Surrealist movement in art and poetry issued
its first public manifesto in 1924. In its purest form
(if we can use such a word for a thing so obscure)
surrealism is simply the dredging up, from the mind's
subconscious level, of a succession of images, unrelated
except in the buried memory of the writer. It is the
same process which is employed in Freudian psycho-
analysis. Here is a surrealist poem translated from
French by David Gascoyne:

> The melancholy of illiterates in the mystery of bottles
> The imperceptible disgust of cartwrights
> Pieces of money in the slender vase
>
> In the cockle-shell of the anvil
>   Dwells the lonely poet
>   Great wheelbarrow of the swamps

It is, of course, quite incomprehensible to the reader who has no clue to the experiences which gave rise to these unconnected and unpunctuated images. They are not symbols, nor are they merely " imagist ", as there is no attempt to relate them to reality. Indeed, in surrealism it is essential that there should be no attempt to organize the phrases which succeed one another without conscious direction like the sequences of a dream. This is a move towards such freedom as was never conceived by the most revolutionary of the Imagists.

The influence of Surrealism in this particular sense was altogether bad. A healthy analysis of one's behaviour and motives (a taking-stock or examination of the conscience) is salutary and sane; but morbid introspection is unhealthy, as is the elevation to an alleged poetic level of symbols which have meaning only for the psycho-analyst.

This extreme surrealism, which is found in French poets like André Breton and Paul Éluard, did not establish itself in England. What we find instead is the use of images drawn from the subconscious mind or arising unbidden from the unconscious. These images the poet contemplates until he finds how to establish connections between them and the thought that is in his mind. Many young poets show this influence: Dylan Thomas, David Gascoyne, Lawrence Durrell, James Kirkup, Paul Dehn, for example. Much of their poetry is therefore obscure. In the poems printed in this anthology, however, the surrealist element adds a romantic richness to the imagery, and the exploration of its sources adds considerably to the reader's enjoyment.

One other influence needs to be mentioned—that

of Gerard Manly Hopkins, poet-Jesuit who died in 1889, leaving behind in the care of Robert Bridges, a body of poetry, none of which had ever been published. In 1918, Bridges brought out a first edition of the poems, but it was barely noticed. It was not until 1930 that a second edition was published. Its impact on poets was tremendous, and imitators sprang up on all sides, carried away by the strange new rhythm and the rich sensuousness of the words and images.

Hopkins called his new rhythm " Sprung Rhythm " and pointed out in what way it was different from " Running Rhythm " which is traditional metre. In the latter the lines are divided into feet, each containing one stressed syllable and one or two unstressed syllables. Sprung Rhythm has a basis of regular stresses, one to a foot as before, but with as many unstressed syllables in between as the poet wishes for his effects. As a result, there may be a verse stress on two successive syllables, with a pause between, or any number of unstressed syllables may have to be hurried through in order to deliver the next stress on time. This is the rhythm of nursery rhymes and broadsheet doggerel. In Hopkins's poetry, however, the strong varied rhythm flows not in single lines, but through whole stanzas, and indeed through the whole poem.

The essence of his poetry is not confined to its rhythm; it is compounded as well of his wealth of original words, his unusually condensed and evocative sentences, and of the beauty of sound which comes out in the copious alliteration, assonance, and rhyme which echo and re-echo in his poetry. The texture of his verse is rich and strange. Its influence on the New-Romantics of the later 1930's is evident in the free rhythm, the rich, sensuous, and sometimes eccentric imagery, and the close-packed expression which makes much of their poetry difficult.

It is clear by now, that in recoil from the Imagists, poets feeling the influence of Symbolism and Surrealism and of Hopkins's poetry, inaugurated a new Romantic movement. The 1939 war gave impetus to it, and it has now reached its climax in the poetry of Edith Sitwell. She stands at the end of one road as T. S. Eliot does at the end of another. In between are many lesser, younger poets, not yet perhaps risen to their full stature. They have their differences in outlook: some write of their own experience, within the limitations of native environment or of domesticity; some have rediscovered the joy of contemplating nature, and in their praise of beauty they praise God who created it; others definitely proclaim their faith in religion. But all of these are alike in a return to lyricism, to a delight in music and rhythm, and to a singleness and simplicity of vision.

Included with these, the reader will find John Masefield, the Poet Laureate, and Walter de la Mare, who, born in 1873, has kept alive, through fifty years of change, the pure essence of poetry. He has never changed. His world is still the world of enchantment unshattered by external cataclysms, and the music of his verse is the most exquisite sound in this century.

III

The poems in this anthology have been selected with one chief aim in view: all had to have something in them which would attract, and not repel or discourage the young student. In addition, a search has been made for poems which refute the objection that modern poetry has no popular appeal because it has no beauty, and particularly no beauty of sound.

It is true that poetry has always been at its lowest in public esteem when it did not primarily aim at pleasing the ear. It was closest to the people when ballads were spoken and sung and *listened to*; and later when Shakespeare's verse was heard in the theatre. The ability to read poetry appears to have killed the popular taste for it, by substituting the eye for the ear. One would like the B.B.C. to add to the good work it is doing on behalf of poetry, by arranging, at popular listening times, programmes of verse read by the poets themselves, and also readings by ordinary people in a variety of accents. One would also like to hear an occasional variety artist speaking some good verse (the applause that greets the straight singing of a classical song is a sign of the fundamental good taste of the average audience, and there is no reason to think that poetry, beautifully spoken, would not be equally well acclaimed). A third hope is in the theatre. That poets have realized this is shown by the number (T. S. Eliot, Norman Nicholson, and Christopher Fry among them) who have recently turned their attention to the writing of poetical drama. Lastly, one has only to listen to Auden's " Funeral Blues " singing itself in the husky voice of a night-club crooner, to realize that poets might do worse than to emulate the Elizabethans, and write the lyrics for our popular songs.

REALISM AND SATIRE

POETS OF THE REACTION

AGAINST GEORGIAN ROMANTICISM

The poets represented in this section belong to the generation which fought in the 1914–18 war. Most of the poems, however, were written during and after the Second World War. While it is possible to see the influence of the Imagists in the freedom of form and in the ordinary, every-day language, there is also evidence of the return to lyricism and more traditional forms.

Reckless

WHAT a fine funeral!
  All six-cylinder cars
Smooth as black velvet,
Fit for a millionaire,
Yet it's only a clerk,
A semi-detached
Who has closed his account,
Paid his last premium,
Safe as a house.
This is his first
Wanton extravagance,
Subtle and rich;
His only adventure.

Richard Church

Gulls and Men

THE naturalists of the Bass Rock
  On this vexatious point agree:
That sea-birds of all sorts that flock
  About the Bass, repeatedly
    Collide in mid-flight,

And neither by design, in play,
  Nor by design in shrewd assault,
But (as these patient watchers say,
  Eyes that are seldom proved at fault)
    By lack of foresight.

Stupidity, which poor and rich
    Hold the recognizance of man,
Precious stupidity, of which
    Let him denude himself who can
        And stand at God's height—

Stupidity that brings to birth
    More, always more, than to the grave,
The burden of all songs on earth,
    And by which men are brave
        And women contrite—

This jewel bandied from a cliff
    By gulls and razor-bills and such!
Where is man's vindication if
    Perfectability's as much
        Bird-right as man-right?

Robert Graves

Saint

THIS Blatant Beast was finally overcome
   And in no secret tourney: wit and fashion
Flocked out and for compassion
Wept as the Red Cross Knight pushed the blade home.

The people danced and sang the pæans due,
Roasting whole oxen on the public spit;
Twelve mountain peaks were lit
With bonfires. Yet their hearts were doubt and rue.

Therefore no grave was deep enough to hold
The Beast, who after days came thrusting out,
Wormy from rump to snout,
His yellow cere-cloth patched with the grave's mould.

Nor could sea hold him: anchored with huge rocks,
He swelled and buoyed them up, paddling ashore
As evident as before
With deep-sea ooze and salty creaking bones.

Lime could not burn him, nor the sulphur-fire:
So often as the good Knight bound him there,
With stink of singeing hair
And scorching flesh the corpse rolled from the pyre.

In the city-gutter would the Beast lie
Praising the Knight for all his valorous deeds:
" Ay, on those water-meads
He slew even me. These death-wounds testify."

The Knight governed that city, a man shamed
And shrunken: for the Beast was over-dead,
With wounds no longer red
But gangrenous and loathsome and inflamed.

Not all the righteous judgments he could utter,
Nor mild laws frame, nor public works repair,
Nor wars wage, in despair,
Could bury that same Beast, crouched in the gutter.

A fresh remembrance-banquet to forestall,
The Knight turned hermit, went without farewell
To a far mountain-cell;
But the Beast followed as his seneschal,

And there drew water for him and hewed wood
With vacant howling laughter; else all day
Noisome with long decay
Sunning himself at the cave's entry stood.

He would bawl to pilgrims for a dole of bread
To feed the sick saint who once vanquished him
With spear so stark and grim;
Would set a pillow of grass beneath his head,
Would fetch him fever-wort from the pool's brim—
And crept into his grave when he was dead.

Robert Graves

The Way Home

EYES had no work to do; mechanical feet
Carried me home down the familiar street,
Past workmen working at the crater. Eyes
Had nothing to do, it seemed, but recognize
The houses a full fortnight now in ruins.

Eyes had no work to do, until to-day
Ears heard from somewhere down that homeward way
A thrush at practice, note by joyous note,
And eyes looked up and saw the speckled throat
Criss-crossed behind green swelling buds of lilac.

Then eyes had other work to do. They saw
Workmen flies in a wound with edges raw;
And a family's knobbed iron bedpost thrust
Through a still avalanche of bricks and dust;
And a staircase carpeted with invitation.

G. Rostrevor Hamilton

The Flaking Pineapple

THE vacant house, grey stone pock-marked and louring,
        In the valley stood,
Through long years patched and tinkered with and garnished
        As architects thought good.

Gate-posts, a Regency addition, flaunted—
        Ridiculous sublime!—
A crinkled pineapple of stone, now flaking,
        To challenge Time.

A weathered board hung out its gothic legend
        Of tarnished gold,
This Old Historic Property, et cetera,
        To be Let (long lease) or Sold.

The garden, cared for once, had run to riot,
        Nettles and grass in flower,
While, straggling, here and there an evening primrose
        Still told the hour.

Beyond it rolled an effortless upland, seeming
        As near its birth
As when the sun and stars first looked upon it,
        Before man came on earth.

Oh, whether take the house, and late redeem it,
        Or, so unkempt, defiled,
Resign this desperate hope, this civilization,
        To the manless wild!

                                        G. Rostrevor Hamilton

Suburban Dream

WALKING the suburbs in the afternoon
In summer when the idle doors stand open
And the air flows through the rooms
Fanning the curtain hems,

You wander through a cool elysium
Of women, schoolgirls, children, garden talks,
With a schoolboy here and there
Conning his history book.

The men are all away in offices,
Committee-rooms, laboratories, banks,
Or pushing cotton goods
In Wick or Ilfracombe.

The massed unanimous absence liberates
The light keys of the piano and sets free
Chopin and everlasting youth,
Now, with the masters gone.

And all things turn to images of peace,
The boy curled over his book, the young girl poised
On the path as if beguiled
By the silence of a wood.

It is a child's dream of a grown-up world.
But soon the brazen evening clocks will bring
The tramp of feet and brisk
Fanfare of motor horns
And the masters come.

Edwin Muir

The Child Dying

UNFRIENDLY friendly universe,
    I pack your stars into my purse,
And bid you, bid you so farewell.
That I can leave you, quite go out,
Go out, go out beyond all doubt,
My father says, is the miracle.

You are so great, and I so small;
I am nothing, you are all.
Being nothing, I can take this way.
Oh, I need neither rise nor fall,
For when I do not move at all
I shall be out of all your day.

It's said some memory may remain
In the other place, grass in the rain,
Light on the land, sun on the sea,
A fleeting grace, a phantom face;
But the world is out. There is no place
Where it and its ghost can ever be.

Father, father, I dread this air
Blown from the far side of despair,
The cold cold corner. What house, what hold,
What hand is there? I look and see
Nothing-filled eternity,
And the great round world grows weak and old.

Hold my hand, oh hold it fast—
I am changing!—until at last
My hand in yours no more will change,
Though yours change on. You here, I there,
So hand in hand, twin-leaved despair:
I did not know death was so strange.

                                        Edwin Muir

A Fable

A CRAZY hunter, following a bear,
    And pressing harder than a man should dare,
Was menaced by a leopard and a lion.
Availed no prayer, no cries to Heaven or Zion,
For he had slain their cubs, and with vile blows,
And welded Sky to Jungle by their woes.

Gazing upon a tree, he swiftly fled.
But in his path the bear with turning tread
Firm hindered the supposed security.
Oh, what to do? How save himself from three?
Dropping his gun, he howled and beat the air;
Then, stretching wide his arms, embraced the bear.
"Save me, sweet beast!" he cried. "Love! Lick my face!"
Which the bear did, returning the embrace.

You know the rest, you know that tightening squeeze.
Only to think, it makes your spirit freeze;
Only to think, it pulls you to the ground,
And makes your blood run cold, your head go round.

Moral: To wicked beasts be straight and fair;
But do not pet them. Face them, and beware!
And never drop your gun to hug a bear.

Herbert Palmer

Summer Rain

A GAINST the window pane
    against the temple of my brain
beat the muffled taps of rain.

Upon the scorch'd and mottled leaves
upon the blench'd and pented sheaves
the land receives

the liquid flood:
water like a blush of blood
returns to the parch'd rood.

The fox has left his fetid hovel
to lick the drenchèd blades of sorrel;
odours rise from thyme and fennel.

The worm in his retreat deep under
the earth's insipid crust
hearing a distant drumming thunder

blindly reveals his upward undulation.
The soil respires as if in emulation
of living things. All elements their maculation

desire and achieve. A warm breath
issues from the nostrils beneath
the mask of death.

Herbert Read

The Case for Miners

SOMETHING goes wrong with my synthetic brain
When I defend the Strikers and explain
My reasons for not blackguarding the Miners.
" *What do you know?*" exclaim my fellow-diners
(Peeling their plovers' eggs or lifting glasses
Of mellowed *Château Rentier* from the table),
" *What do you know about the working classes?*"

I strive to hold my own; but I'm unable
To state the case succinctly. Indistinctly
I mumble about World-Emancipation,
Standards of Living, Nationalization
Of Industry; until they get me tangled
In superficial details; goad me on
To unconvincing vagueness. When we've wrangled
From soup to savoury, my temper's gone.

" *Why should a miner earn six pounds a week?*
Leisure! They'd only spend it in a bar!
Standard of life! You'll never teach them Greek,
Or make them more contented than they are!"
That's how my port-flushed friends discuss the Strike.
And that's the reason why I shout and splutter.
And that's the reason why I'd almost like
To see them hawking matches in the gutter.

Siegfried Sassoon

At the Cenotaph

I SAW the Prince of Darkness, with his Staff,
   Standing bare-headed by the Cenotaph:
Unostentatious and respectful, there
He stood, and offered up the following prayer.
   " Make them forget, O Lord, what this Memorial
      Means; their discredited ideas revive;
   Breed new belief that War is purgatorial
      Proof of the pride and power of being alive;
   Men's biologic urge to readjust
      The map of Europe, Lord of Hosts, increase;
   Lift up their hearts in large destructive lust;
      And crown their heads with blind vindictive Peace."
The Prince of Darkness to the Cenotaph
Bowed. As he walked away I heard him laugh.

Siegfried Sassoon

A Flower Has Opened

A FLOWER has opened in my heart. . . .
What flower is this, what flower of spring,
What simple, secret thing?
It is the peace that shines apart,
The peace of daybreak skies that bring
Clear song and 'wild swift wing.

Heart's miracle of inward light,
What powers unknown have sown your seed
And your perfection freed? . . .
O flower within me wondrous white,
I know you only as my need
And my unsealèd sight.

Siegfried Sassoon

Since Thought Is Life

SINCE thought is life, God's martyrdoms were good,
And saints are trumps, no matter what they did.
Therefore I celebrate Sebastian's blood,
And glory with Lorenzo on his grid,
And likewise with all victims, bruised by boulders,
Stabbed by sadistic swords, on pikes impaled,
Who propped their Paradise on bleeding shoulders
And bred tumultuous pomps when princes failed.

Thus for their murdered Master—thus for his dreamed
Utopia—from a crookèd Roman cross,
Heavenward on crimson clouds their conquest streamed
To touch His lips in life-redeeming loss.

Siegfried Sassoon

Field-Glasses

THOUGH buds still speak in hints
  And frozen ground has set the flints
As fast as precious stones
And birds perch on the boughs, silent as cones,

Suddenly waked from sloth
Young trees put on a ten years' growth
And stones double their size,
Drawn nearer through field-glasses' greater eyes.

Why I borrow their sight
Is not to give small birds a fright
Creeping up close by inches;
I make the trees come, bringing tits and finches.

I lift a field itself
As lightly as I might a shelf,
And the rooks do not rage
Caught for a moment in my crystal cage.

And while I stand and look,
Their private lives an open book,
I feel so privileged
My shoulders prick, as though they were half-fledged.

Andrew Young

The Shepherd's Hut

THE smear of blue peat smoke
  That staggered on the wind and broke,
The only sign of life,
Where was the shepherd's wife,
Who left those flapping clothes to dry,
Taking no thought for her family?
For, as they bellied out
And limbs took shape and waved about,
I thought, she little knows
That ghosts are trying on her children's clothes.

Andrew Young

REALISTS OF THE 1930's

POETRY OF THE COMMON MAN

These are the poets who began to be heard from 1930 onwards. They include the social and political propagandists, the witty intellectuals whose satire, though apparently flippant, is nevertheless deeply and sincerely felt. These are the poets who caused a minor revolution in the world of poetry, and even succeeded in penetrating the consciousness of the average non-reader of poetry. All Art develops, not by slow, almost imperceptible stages, but by shocks and starts. Auden and Co. administered one of these salutary shocks.

The Unknown Citizen

(To JS/07/M/378
This Marble Monument
Is Erected by the State)

H E was found by the Bureau of Statistics to be
    One against whom there was no official complaint,
And all the reports on his conduct agree
That, in the modern sense of an old-fashioned word, he was
    a saint,
For in everything he did he served the Greater Community.
Except for the War till the day he retired
He worked in a factory and never got fired,
But satisfied his employers, Fudge Motors Inc.
Yet he wasn't a scab or odd in his views,
For his Union reports that he paid his dues,
(Our report on his Union shows it was sound)
And our Social Psychology workers found
That he was popular with his mates and liked a drink.
The Press are convinced that he bought a paper every day
And that his reactions to advertisements were normal in every
    way.
Policies taken out in his name prove that he was fully insured,
And his Health-card shows he was once in hospital but left it
    cured.
Both Producers Research and High-Grade Living declare
He was fully sensible to the advantages of the Instalment Plan
And had everything necessary to the Modern Man,
A phonograph, a radio, a car and a frigidaire.
Our researchers into Public Opinion are content
That he held the proper opinions for the time of year;
When there was peace, he was for peace; when there was war,
    he went.

He was married and added five children to the population,
Which our Eugenist says was the right number for a parent
    of his generation,
And öur teachers report that he never interfered with their
    education.
Was he free? Was he happy? The question is absurd:
Had anything been wrong, we should certainly have heard.

W. H. Auden

Musée des Beaux Arts

ABOUT suffering they were never wrong,
    The Old Masters: how well they understood
Its human position; how it takes place
While someone else is eating or opening a window or just
    walking dully along;
How, when the aged are reverently, passionately waiting
For the miraculous birth, there always must be
Children who did not specially want it to happen, skating
On a pond at the edge of the wood:
They never forgot
That even the dreadful martyrdom must run its course
Anyhow in a corner, some untidy spot
Where the dogs go on with their doggy life and the torturer's
    horse
Scratches its innocent behind on a tree.

In Brueghel's *Icarus*, for instance: how everything turns away
Quite leisurely from the disaster; the ploughman may
Have heard the splash, the forsaken cry,
But for him it was not an important failure; the sun shone
As it had to on the white legs disappearing into the green
Water; and the expensive delicate ship that must have seen
Something amazing, a boy falling out of the sky,
Had somewhere to get to and sailed calmly on.

W. H. Auden

O *What Is That Sound?*

O WHAT is that sound which so thrills the ear
    Down in the valley drumming, drumming?
Only the scarlet soldiers, dear,
  The soldiers coming.

O what is that light I see flashing so clear
    Over the distance brightly, brightly?
Only the sun on their weapons, dear,
  As they step lightly.

O what are they doing with all that gear,
    What are they doing this morning, this morning?
Only their usual manoeuvres, dear,
  Or perhaps a warning.

O why have they left the road down there,
    Why are they suddenly wheeling, wheeling?
Perhaps a change in their orders, dear.
  Why are you kneeling?

O haven't they stopped for the doctor's care,
    Haven't they reined their horses, their horses?
Why, they are none of them wounded, dear,
  None of these forces.

O is it the parson they want, with white hair,
    Is it the parson, is it, is it?
No, they are passing his gateway, dear,
  Without a visit.

O it must be the farmer who lives so near.
    It must be the farmer so cunning, so cunning?
They have passed the farmyard already, dear,
  And now they are running.

O where are you going? Stay with me here!
    Were the vows you swore deceiving, deceiving?
No, I promised to love you, dear,
    But I must be leaving.

O it's broken the lock and splintered the door,
    O it's the gate where they're turning, turning;
Their boots are heavy on the floor
    And their eyes are burning.

                        W. H. Auden

Refugee Blues

SAY this city has ten million souls,
    Some are living in mansions, some are living in holes;
Yet there's no place for us, my dear, yet there's no place for
    us.

Once we had a country and we thought it fair,
Look in the atlas and you'll find it there;
We can never go there now, my dear, we can never go there
    now.

The consul banged the table and said:
"If you've no passport, you're officially dead";
But we are still alive, my dear, but we are still alive.

Down in the churchyard there stands an old yew,
Every spring it flowers anew;
Old passports can't do that, my dear, old passports can't do
    that.

Went to a committee; they offered me a chair,
Told me politely to come back next year;
But where shall we go to-day, my dear, but where shall we
    go to-day?

Came to a public meeting; the speaker got up and said:
" If we let them in, they will steal our daily bread ";
He was talking of you and me, my dear, he was talking of
    you and me.

Heard a noise like thunder rumbling in the sky,
It was Hitler over Europe saying: " They must die!"
O we were in his mind, my dear, O we were in his mind.

Saw a poodle in a jacket, fastened with a pin,
Saw a door open and a cat let in:
But they weren't German Jews, my dear, but they weren't
    German Jews.

Went down to the harbour and stood upon the quay,
Saw the fish swimming as if they were free;
Only ten feet away, my dear, only ten feet away.

Walked into a wood; there were birds in the trees,
They had no politicians and sang at their ease;
They weren't the human race, my dear, they weren't the
    human race.

Dreamt I saw a building with a thousand floors,
A thousand windows and a thousand doors;
Not one of them was ours, my dear, not one of them was
    ours.

Ran down to the station to catch the express,
Asked for two tickets to Happiness;
But every coach was full, my dear, but every coach was full.

Stood on a great plain in the falling snow,
Ten thousand soldiers marched to and fro,
Looking for you and me, my dear, looking for you and me.

                                                              W. H. Auden

In Westminster Abbey

LET me take this other glove off
    As the *vox humana* swells,
And the beauteous fields of Eden
    Bask beneath the Abbey bells.
Here, where England's statesmen lie,
Listen to a lady's cry.

Gracious Lord, oh bomb the Germans.
    Spare their women for Thy Sake,
And if that is not too easy
    We will pardon Thy Mistake.
But, gracious Lord, whate'er shall be,
Don't let anyone bomb me.

Keep our Empire undismembered
    Guide our Forces by Thy Hand,
Gallant blacks from far Jamaica,
    Honduras and Togoland;
Protect them Lord in all their fights,
And, even more, protect the whites.

Think of what our Nation stands for,
    Books from Boots' and country lanes,
Free speech, free passes, class distinction,
    Democracy and proper drains.
Lord, put beneath Thy special care
One-eighty-nine Cadogan Square.

Although dear Lord I am a sinner,
    I have done no major crime;
Now I'll come to Evening Service
    Whensoever I have time.
So, Lord, reserve for me a crown,
And do not let my shares go down.

I will labour for Thy Kingdom,
    Help our lads to win the war,
Send white feathers to the cowards
    Join the Women's Army Corps,
Then wash the Steps around Thy Throne
In the Eternal Safety Zone.

Now I feel a little better,
    What a treat to hear Thy Word,
Where the bones of leading statesmen,
    Have so often been interr'd.
And now, dear Lord, I cannot wait
Because I have a luncheon date.

John Betjeman

The Birth of Christ

NOW that the season was approaching
    Of His long-expected birth,
Like a bridegroom from his chamber
He emerged upon our earth

Clinging close to His beloved
Whom He brought along with Him.
While the gracious Mary placed them
In a manger damp and dim.

Amongst the animals that round it
At that season stretched their limbs,
Men were singing songs of gladness
And the angels chanting hymns,

To celebrate the wondrous marriage
By whose bond such two were tied,
But the wee God in the manger
He alone made moan and cried;

Tears were the jewels of the dowry
Which the bride with her had brought.
And the Mother gazed upon them
Nearly fainting at the thought.

The tears of Man in God alone,
The joy of God in men was seen.
Two things so alien to each other,
Or to the rule, had never been.

Roy Campbell

Washing Day

AMONGST the rooftop chimneys where the breezes
   Their dizzy choreography design,
Pyjamas, combinations, and chemises
Inflate themselves and dance upon the line.
Drilled by a loose disorder and abandon,
They belly and explode, revolve and swing,
As fearless of the precipice they stand on
As if there were religion in a string.
Annexing with their parachute invasion
The intimate behaviour of our life,
They argue, or embrace with kind persuasion,
And parody our dalliance or our strife.
We change ideas and moods like shirts or singlets,
Which, having shed, they rise to mock us still;
And the wind laughs and shakes her golden ringlets
To set them independent of our will.
They curtsey and collapse, revolve and billow—
A warning that, when least aware we lie,
The dreams are incubated in our pillow
That animate its chrysalis to fly.

Roy Campbell

The Stand-To

AUTUMN met me to-day as I walked over Castle Hill.
    The wind that had set our corn by the ears was blowing
    still:
Autumn, who takes the leaves and the long days, crisped the
    air
With a tang of action, a taste of death; and the wind blew
    fair   •

From the east for men and barges massed on the other side—
Men maddened by numbers or stolid by nature, they have
    their pride
As we in work and children, but now a contracting will
Crumples their meek petitions and holds them poised to kill.

Last night a Stand-To was ordered. Thirty men of us here
Came out to guard the star-lit village—my men who wear
Unwitting the seasons' beauty, the received truth of the spade—
Roadmen, farm labourers, masons, turned to another trade.

A dog barked over the fields, the candle stars put a sheen
On the rifles ready, the sandbags fronded with evergreen:
The dawn wind blew, the stars winked out on the posts
    where we lay,
The order came, Stand Down, and thirty went away.

Since a cold wind from Europe blows back the words in my
    teeth,
Since autumn shortens the days and the odds against our
    death,
And the harvest moon is waxing, and the high tides threaten
    harm,
Since last night may be the last night all thirty men go home,

I write this verse to record the men who have watched with
    me—
Spot who is good at darts, Squibby at repartee,
Mark and Cyril, the dead shots, Ralph with a ploughman's
    gait,
Gibson, Harris and Long, old hands for the barricade,

Whiller the lorry-driver, Francis and Rattlesnake,
Fred and Charl and Stan—these nights I have lain awake
And thought of my thirty men and the autumn wind that
    blows
The apples down too early and shatters the autumn rose.

Destiny, History, Duty, Fortitude, Honour—all
The words of the politicians seem too big or too small
For the ragtag fighters of lane and shadow, the love that has
    grown
Familiar as working-clothes, faithful as bone to bone.

Blow, autumn wind, upon orchard and rose! Blow leaves
    along
Our lanes, but sing through me for the lives that are worth a
    song!
Narrowing days have darkened the vistas that hurt my eyes,
But pinned to the heart of darkness a tattered fire-flag flies.

                                                C. Day Lewis

Will It Be So Again?

WILL it be so again
      That the brave, the gifted are lost from view,
And empty, scheming men
Are left in peace their lunatic age to renew?
Will it be so again?

Must it be always so
That the best are chosen to fall and sleep
Like seeds, and we too slow
In claiming the earth they quicken, and the old usurpers reap
What they could not sow?

Will it be so again—
The jungle code and the hypocrite gesture?
A poppy wreath for the slain
And a cut-throat world for the living? that stale imposture
Played on us once again?

Will it be as before—
Peace, with no heart or mind to ensue it,
Guttering down to war
Like a libertine to his grave? We should not be surprised:
    we knew it
Happen before.

Shall it be so again?
Call not upon the glorious dead
To be your witnesses then.
The living alone can nail to their promise the ones who said
It shall not be so again.

                             C. Day Lewis

Word over All

NOW when drowning imagination clutches
    At old loves drifting away,
Splintered highlights, hope capsized—a wrecked world's
Flotsam—what can I say
To cheer the abysmal gulfs, the crests that lift not
To any land in sight?
How shall the sea-waif, who lives from surge to surge, chart
Current and reef aright?

Always our time's ghost-guise of impermanence
Daunts me: whoever I meet,
Wherever I stand, a shade of parting lengthens
And laps around my feet.
But now, the heart-sunderings, the real migrations—
Millions fated to flock
Down weeping roads to mere oblivion—strike me
Dumb as a rooted rock.

I watch when searchlights set the low cloud smoking
Like acid on metal: I start
At sirens, sweat to feel a whole town wince
And thump, a terrified heart,
Under the bomb-strokes. These, to look back on, are
A few hours' unrepose:
But the roofless old, the child beneath the debris—
How can I speak for those?

Busy the preachers, the politicians weaving
Voluble charms around
This ordeal, conjuring a harvest that shall spring from
Our hearts' all-harrowed ground.
I, who chose to be caged with the devouring
Present, must hold its eye
Where blaze ten thousand farms and fields unharvested,
And hearts, steel-broken, die.

Yet words there must be, wept on the cratered present,
To gleam beyond it:
Never was cup so mortal but poets with mild
Everlastings have crowned it.
See wavelets and wind-blown shadows of leaves on a stream
How they ripple together,
As life and death intermarried—you cannot tell
One from another.

Our words like poppies love the maturing field,
But form no harvest:
May lighten the innocent's pang, or paint the dreams
Where guilt is unharnessed.
Dark over all, absolving all, is hung
Death's vaulted patience:
Words are to set man's joy and suffering there
In constellations.

We speak of what we know, but what we have spoken
Truly we know not—
Whether our good may tarnish, our grief to far
Centuries glow not.
The Cause shales off, the Humankind stands forth
A mightier presence,
Flooded by dawn's pale courage, rapt in eve's
Rich acquiescence.

C. Day Lewis

Prayer before Birth

I AM not yet born; O hear me.
   Let not the bloodsucking bat or the rat or the stoat or
   the
   club-footed ghoul come near me.

I am not yet born, console me.
I fear that the human race may with tall walls wall me,
   with strong drugs dope me, with wise lies lure me,
      on black racks rack me, in blood-baths roll me.

I am not yet born; provide me
With water to dandle me, grass to grow for me, trees to talk
   to me, sky to sing to me, birds and a white light
      in the back of my mind to guide me.

I am not yet born; forgive me
For the sins that in me the world shall commit, my words
   when they speak me, my thoughts when they think me,
     my treason engendered by traitors beyond me,
       my life when they murder by means of my
        hands, my death when they live me.

I am not yet born; rehearse me
In the parts I must play and the cues I must take when
   old men lecture me, bureaucrats hector me, mountains
     frown at me, lovers laugh at me, the white
       waves call me to folly and the desert calls
        me to doom and the beggar refuses
         my gift and my children curse me.

I am not yet born; O hear me,
Let not the man who is beast or who thinks he is God
   come near me.

I am not yet born; O fill me
With strength against those who would freeze my
   humanity, would dragoon me into a lethal automaton,
     would make me a cog in a machine, a thing with
       one face, a thing, and against all those
        who would dissipate my entirety, would
         blow me like thistledown hither and
          thither or hither and thither
           like water held in the
            hands would spill me.

Let them not make me a stone and let them not spill me.
Otherwise kill me.

                    Louis MacNeice

Flight of the Heart

HEART, my heart, what will you do?
    There are five lame dogs and one deaf-mute
All of them with demands on you.

    I will build myself a copper tower
    With four ways out and no way in
    But mine the glory, mine the power.

And what if the tower should shake and fall
With three sharp taps and one big bang?
What would you do with yourself at all?

    I would go in the cellar and drink the dark
    With two quick sips and one long pull,
    Drunk as a lord and gay as a lark.

But what when the cellar roof caves in
With one blue flash and nine old bones?
How, my heart, will you save your skin?

    I will go back where I belong
    With one foot first and both eyes blind,
    I will go back where I belong
    In the fore-being of mankind.

Louis MacNeice

Spring Voices

THE small householder now comes out warily
    Afraid of the barrage of sun that shouts cheerily,
Spring is massing forces, birds wink in air,
The battlemented chestnuts volley green fire,
The pigeons banking on the wind, the hoots of cars,
Stir him to run wild, gamble on horses, buy cigars;

Joy lies before him to be ladled and lapped from his hand—
Only that behind him, in the shade of his villa, memories
  stand
Breathing on his neck and muttering that all this has happened
  before,
Keep the wind out, cast no clout, try no unwarranted jaunts
  untried before,
But let the spring slide by nor think to board its car
For it rides West where the tangles of scrap-iron are;
Do not walk, these voices say, between the bucking clouds
  alone
Or you may loiter into a suddenly howling crater, or fall,
  jerked back, garrotted by the sun.

          Louis MacNeice

September Evening, 1938

A S the golden grass burns out
  In a cooling ash of dew
The lovers disembrace
And face the evening view.

The long plain down
Shaped like a thigh
Slopes towards the sea,
And away up in the sky

Too small to be heard
A plane like a silver spark
Bright in the sun's last rays
Drifts eastward into the dark;

A single stack of hay
In the valley at their feet
Like a primitive small church
Looks simple, strong, and neat;

Inside a wattled fold
A flock of sheep
Stand, stir, or lie
Fleece against fleece asleep;

Lights in the bungalow,
A constant hum of cars;
Mallow flowers in the grass;
One or two stars.

With the fading day
All has grown clear:
That everything is vital
And infinitely dear.

Looking round, the girl thinks
" How precious to me
My home and my work and each thing
I can touch and can see,

George's navy-blue suit,
And my white linen dress,
And the way that his eyebrows grow—
This is my happiness!"

And he, clasping her hand,
More grave than before,
Says, " Yes, I will fight
(If there is to be a war)

For all that has gone to make
Us, and this day."
Then arm in arm along the path
Silent they saunter away.

William Plomer

To Poets and Airmen

(Dedicated to Michael Jones in his life, and now in his memory)

THINKERS and airmen—all such
  Friends and pilots upon the edge
Of the skies of the future—much
    You require a bullet's eye of courage
    To fly through this age.

The paper brows are winged and helmeted,
    The blind ankles bound to a white road
Streaming through a night of lead
    Where cities explode,
    Fates unload

Hatred burning, in small parcels,
    Outrage against social lies,
Hearts breaking against past refusals
    Of men to show small mercies
    To men. Now death replies
Releasing new, familiar devils.

And yet, before you throw away your childhood,
    With the lambs pasturing in flaxen hair,
    To plunge into this iron war,
Remember for a flash the wild good
    Drunkenness where
    You abandoned future care,

And then forget. Become what
    Things require. The expletive word.
    The all-night-long screeching metal bird.
And all of time shut down in one shot
    Of night, by a gun uttered.

Stephen Spender

The Air Raid across the Bay

I

ABOVE the dead flat sea
    And watching rocks of black coast
Across the bay, the high
Searchlights probe the centre of the sky
Their ends fusing in cones of light
For a brilliant instant held up
Then shattered like a cup.

They rub white rules through leaden dark,
Projecting tall phantom
Masts with swaying derricks
Above the sea's broad level decks.

They slide triangles and parallels
Of experimental theorems,
Proving the hypothesis
Of death, on wasted surfaces
Of measureless blank distances.

II

But through their gliding light-streams,
    An invisible ragged sound
Moves, trailed by two distraught beams.
    A thudding falls from remote cones
And pink sequins wink from a shot-silk screen.

    Seeds of killing drop on cells of sleep
Which hug these promontories like dark-brown wrinkles.

Fingers pick away
Human minds from hollow skulls,

III

The shining ladders slant
Up to the god of war
Exalted on those golden stilts
And riding in his car
Of a destroying star.

But the waves clucking in the rocks
And the sacred standing corn
Brittle, and swaying with metallic clicks,
Their secret wealth lock
In an elemental magic
Of ripeness, which mocks
The nails through flesh torn.

Stephen Spender

NEW ROMANTIC MOVEMENT

EMBRACING SYMBOLISM
AND SURREALISM

This group of younger poets, in reaction against the realism and the unemotional, everyday language of the previous generation, withdrew into themselves. In seeking to express the unresolved complexities of their experience, they had resort to allusive, symbolic, evocative language, which is difficult to interpret. For this reason, the poets of this period removed poetry farther away from the comprehension of the people than it had ever been before. But these poets, too, as they have grown older, have achieved greater clarity of vision, and therefore greater lucidity of expression.

From: *Calamiterror*

1

THE English coast shivers and the American meadow faints;
The Rhone and the Rhine run mellowing with promised
   horror;
The Welsh mountain weeps and the Cumberland fell weeps;
London lies like a huge rot along the Thames, and Rome
Roars. O Spain, my golden red, she tears the rot out,
The Franco gangs that furrow in her heart. See how she
   stands,
Her Madrid middle growing vague with ravage,
Labouring to let out liberty, with the rat and the rot at her
   heart.

2

I remember again the three women weeping in Irun's ruins,
Whose tears will wash the Rhone and Rhine and whose grief
Thrust up like crystal towers the architecture of Time.
I see England
With the underground mines run bleeding along her like
   wounds,
I hear the great Lancastrian shafts delivering sounds
Of sorrow and appeal, or watch the factory stacks
Like hands for charity, or fallen, clenched.

3

The centre of my heart like a red tree
Puts forth a hand and indicates the common red rose;
Which when I take lifts its petals like tongues
Articulating red; speaks of privations, poverty,
Duplicity, oppressions, camouflaged collusions;
And I observe that every move of its lips leaves blood.
What flower then shall the red tree in my heart wear
But the red tongues of the rose, which speak and bleed?

4

O Asturias Wyoming and Wales, I see the fuchsia
Remembering man has a crimson heart and I remember,
Hang out my fuchsia here. Your fuchsia, Asturias,
Spreading like sun over Spain shall be soon in bloom:
The dead is dead, but he gives and not takes his poppy,
His hammer his hand and his badge his blood.
It is already time to triumph, for tears and blood like time
Take tears and blood as time takes time to make good.

5

I see the swan's breast run like the pelican's red
To feed the crowded myriad her human,
I see the large parasites that dilate like leech
Torn, with war and agony, from my mother world's front.
But the whipporwill wends his way through the Wyoming
    woods
When the leopard, lying low, awaits, or the lion
Roars.   And my mother world, with bomb holes in her
    bosom,
Goes gradually on, with the myriad of me at her breast.

George Barker

Lament for a Sailor

HERE, where the night is clear as sea-water
   And stones are white and the sticks are spars,
Swims on a windless, mackerel tide
The dolphin moon in a shoal of stars.

Here, in the limbo, where moths are spinners
And clouds like hulls drift overhead,
Move we must for our colder comfort,
I the living and you the dead.

Each on our way, my ghost, my grayling,
You to the water, the land for me;
I am the fat-knuckled, noisy diver
But you are the quietest fish in the sea.

Paul Dehn

Habitué

GO home, go home, there is nothing for you here
   Already, now, beyond the cocktail-bar
In moss-green chairs, like crocuses appearing,
The pretty ones are pairing.
Touch the dove necktie, smooth the ebbing hair;
Stare,
Stare, if you must;
But call for hat and stick, before the tear
Lipping your pink and pug-dog eye
Proclaims a loneliness and lust
That no one, now, could wish to satisfy.

There is nothing for you here. Go home, go home
To the rococo mirror in your room
Where egg-shell beauty, as the mornings pass,
Has mottled in the glass.

Unstopper talc and turtle-oil and cream;
Dream,
Dream, if you will,
That once, crow's-feet ago, there was a time
When the fair sought you as now you seek the fair.
Tip the grave bar-boy. Pay the bill,
And walk alone under the evening air.

Paul Dehn

On Ithaca Standing

TREAD softly, for here you stand
  On miracle ground, boy:
A breath would cloud this water of glass,
Honey, bush, berry and swallow.
This rock, then, is more pastoral, than
Arcadia is, Illyria was.

Here the cold spring lilts on sand.
The temperature of the toad
Swallowing under a stone whispers: " Diamonds,
Boy, diamonds, and a juice of minerals!"
Be a saint here, dig for foxes, and water,
Mere water springs in the bones of the hands.

Turn from the hearth of the hero. Think:
Other men have their problems, I this:
The heart's dark anvil and the crucifix
Are one, have hammered and shall hammer
A nail of flesh, me to an island cross,
Where the kestrel's arrow falls only,
The green sea licks.

Lawrence Durrell

Pieta

HER heart with grief is singular as the sky
    That never was so dark. His body sags
Like a fisherman's dripping net, a burden
For all its thinness. The limbs are unruly
As a new-born calf's. O lifeless liveliness
That once moved with such purpose on the earth!
Woman, it is proper you should weep,
Weep for the voice you knew, the step
Familiar on the path, the youth you tended
Growing so tall and a pride. How can you know
How small your Jesus is, the man in man,
Figure on wood and flesh in time?
You are deprived of our advantage:
Wise after the event, we know that Christ
Triumphant is no theme for grief:
Mary, mother, our tears are for you.

Clifford Dyment

The Divided Life Re-Lived

ONCE again the light refracted through the dusty crimson
    air
Leaves the spaces of the evening blurred and bare.
Bats that flicker round the edges of the square Victorian lawn
Symbolise the bourgeois souls from life withdrawn.

Now the nightingale arouses us upon the withered tree
With its disappointing, moving melody,
And against the chalky purple thrown by distant main-road
    arcs
Flow the tired suburban leaves like mouldy sparks.

Here the mower furred with grass like filings round a magnet's
    pole,
Teacups left for ants to make our fortunes droll;
While we sit and try to think that everything is not too late—
Sparrows sitting on the sad outfield of fate.

Once and only once we were in touch with brutal, bloody life
When we got in or kept out of global strife;
And in desert or in dockyard met our coarser fellow men,
Wielding friendly gun or scrubber, not our pen.

How we innocently thought that we should be alone no more,
Linked in death or revolution as in war.
How completely we have slipped into the same old world of
    cod,
Our companions Henry James or cats or God.

Waiting for the evening as the time of passion and of verse,
Vainly hoping that at both we shan't get worse:
While outside the demon scientists and rulers of the land
Pile the bombs like busy crabs pile balls of sand.

And the best that we can wish for is that still the moon will
    rise
Enigmatic, cracked and yellow to men's eyes,
And illuminate the manuscripts of poems that foretold
All the ruin and survival of the old.

Roy Fuller

A Tough Generation

TO grow unguided at a time when none
  Are sure where they should plant their sprig of trust;
When sunshine has no special mission to endow
With gold the rustic rose, which will run wild
And ramble from the garden to the wood
To train itself to climb the trunks of trees
If the old seedsman die and suburbs care
For sentimental cottage-flowers no more;
To grow up in a wood of rotted trees
In which it is not known which tree will be
First to disturb the silent sultry grove
With crack of doom, dead crackling and dread roar:
Will be infallibly to learn that first
One always owes a duty to oneself—
This much at least is certain: one must live.
And one may reach, without having to search
For much more lore than this, a shrewd maturity,
Equipped with adult aptitude to ape
All customary cant and current camouflage;
Nor be a whit too squeamish where the soul's concerned,
But hold out for the best black market price for it
Should need remind one that one has to live.
Yet just as sweetly, where no markets are,
An unkempt rose may for a season still
Trust its own beauty, and disclose its heart
Even to the woodland shade, and as in sacrifice
Renounce its ragged petals one by one.

David Gascoyne

Café Au Lait

WE talked of war with light and easy lips,
jesting upon our action, this or that,
if it came to the last, and while we chattered
we drank our coffee in delicious sips
and watched the soft, contented café cat.

But then the woman in the wicker chair
cried Havoc! and suddenly I was afire
because I saw, under the skirts of light,
the corpses of our laughter and delight
smashed and dismembered, bloodily bespattered
across the red carpet . . .

And still the solemn stare
of all the sleepy cats in Oxfordshire.

Seán Jennett

Christ's Cross Grows Wings

CHRIST'S cross grows wings, and though the smothering
clouds
obscure the curse, the raging out of heaven
roars through the flowering faces and the ravelled mind;
and the carelessness of death is the only haven,
the only refuge from the dangerous skies.

We live in a time of madness, and the plague
infects the restricted nerve and spins the heart
to iron heat; and holds the heaving day
fixed in the agony of the unhealing hurt
that festers for the foolish and the wise.

With Christ's man split by the unmourning hate
love flags and falls; and the bitter sea moves in
to claim the corpse for its distorting wave:
while broken from his usurped symbol One
    feels in his wounds the gangrene's agonies.

Seán Jennett

The Martyr

THESE are my hands which wait
    With severed wrists
For something to create,
For someone to restore,
Although the hour be late,
Their strength of yore.

This is my head which bleeds,
With lips that gasp
Their human fears and needs,
And black, contorted face:
But no one helps or heeds
Gasp or grimace.

This is my heart which lies
Plucked from my breast:
And still my body cries
" O join the vital thread
Without which each part lies
Lost, dark, and dead ".

Francis King

From: The Drowned Sailor

. . . . .

ONCE he lay drugged in
  a southern ocean,
and for nine
weeks dreamed,
standing with his arms above his head

And once he penetrated
one long winter
into a dim fiord where a miracle
seemed always on the point of happen:
and there for many months he lay
aslant in ice,
his spread hair
transfixed, and in his arms
a tree.

But everywhere submerged,
encountering
nothing, nothing

. . . . . .

James Kirkup

Bird

O BIRD that was my vision,
  my love, my dream that flew
over the famine-folded rocks,
the sky's reflected snow.

O bird that found and fashioned me,
that brought me from the land
safe in her singing cage of bone,
the webbed wings of her hand.

She took me to the topmost air,
curled in the atom of her eye,
and there I saw an island rise
out of the empty sea.

And falling there she set me down
naked on soil that knew no plough,
and loveless, speechless, I beheld
the world's beginning grow.

And there I slew her for my bread
and in her feathers dressed;
and there I raised a paradise
from the seed in her dead breast.

                                        Laurie Lee

Christmas Landscape

TO-NIGHT the wind gnaws
      with teeth of glass,
the jackdaw shivers
in caged branches of iron,
the stars have talons.

There is hunger in the mouth
of vole and badger,
silver agonies of breath
in the nostril of the fox,
ice on the rabbit's paw.

To-night has no moon,
no food for the pilgrim;
the fruit tree is bare,
the rose bush a thorn
and the ground bitter with stones.

But the mole sleeps, and the hedgehog
lies curled in a womb of leaves,
the bean and the wheat-seed
hug their germs in the earth
and the stream moves under the ice.

To-night there is no moon,
but a new star opens
like a silver trumpet over the dead.
To-night in a nest of ruins
the blessed babe is laid.

And the fir tree warms to a bloom of candles,
the child lights his lantern,
stares at his tinselled toy;
our hearts and hearths
smoulder with live ashes.

In the blood of our grief
the cold earth is suckled,
in our agony the womb
convulses its seed,
in the cry of anguish
the child's first breath is born.

Laurie Lee

Autumn Day

GOING out, those bold days,
O what a gallery-roar of trees and gale-wash
Of leaves abashed me, what a shudder and shore
Of bladdery shadows dashed on windows ablaze,
What hedge-shingle seething, what vast lime-splashes
Of light clouting the land. Never had I seen
Such a running-over of clover, such tissue sheets
Of cloud poled asunder by sun, such plunges

And thunder-load of fun. Trees, grasses, wings—all
On a hone of wind sluiced and sleeked one way,
Smooth and close as the pile of a pony's coat,
But, in a moment, smoke-slewed, glared, squinted back
And up like sticking bones shockingly unkinned.
How my heart, like all these, was silk and thistle
By turns, how it fitted and followed the stiff lifts
And easy falls of them, or, like that bird above me,
No longer crushing against cushions of air,
Hung in happy apathy, waiting for wind-rifts.
Who could not dance on, and be dandled by, such a day
Of loud expansion? when every flash and shout
Took the hook of the mind and reeled out the eye's line
Into whips and whirl-spools of light, when every ash-shoot
        shone
Like a weal and was gone in the gloom of the wind's lash.
Who could not feel it? the uplift and total subtraction
Of breath as, now bellying, now in abeyance,
The gust poured up from the camp's throat below, bringing
Garbled reports of guns and bugle-notes,
But, gullible, then drank them back again.
And I, dryly shuffling the scurf of leaves
Fleeing like scuffled toast, was host to all these things;
In me were the spoon-swoops of wind, in me too
The rooks dying and settling like tea-leaves over the trees;
And, rumbling on rims of rhyme, mine were the haycarts
        home-creeping
Leaving the rough hedge-cheeks long-strawed and streaked
        with their weeping.

                                                        W. R. Rodgers

Dawn Raid

(Among those killed in the Dawn Raid was a Man Aged a Hundred)

WHEN the morning was waking over the war
He put on his clothes and stepped out and he died,
The locks yawned loose and a blast blew them wide,
He dropped where he loved on the burst pavement of stone
And the funeral grains of the slaughtered floor.
Tell his street on its back he stopped a sun
And the craters of his eyes grew springshoots and fire
When all the keys shot from the locks, and rang.
Dig no more for the chains of his grey-haired heart.
The heavenly ambulance drawn by a wound
Assembling waits for the spade's ring on the cage.
O keep his bones away from that common cart,
The morning is flying on the wings of his age
And a hundred storks perch on the sun's right hand.

Dylan Thomas

To Others Than You

FRIEND by enemy I call you out.

You with a bad coin in your socket,
You my friend there with a winning air
Who palmed the lie on me when you looked
Brassily at my shyest secret,
Enticed with twinkling bits of the eye
Till the sweet tooth of my love bit dry,
Rasped at last, and I stumbled and sucked,
Whom now I conjure to stand as thief
In the memory worked by mirrors,
With unforgettably smiling act,
Quickness of hand in the velvet glove
And my whole heart under your hammer,

Were once such a creature, so gay and frank
A desireless familiar
I never thought to utter or think
While you displaced a truth in the air,

That though I loved them for their faults
As much as for their good,
My friends were enemies on stilts
With their heads in a cunning cloud.

Dylan Thomas

Fern Hill

Now as I was young and easy under the apple boughs
About the lilting house and happy as the grass was green,
    The night above the dingle starry,
        Time let me hail and climb
    Golden in the heydays of his eyes,
And honoured among wagons I was prince of the apple towns
And once below a time I lordly had the trees and leaves
        Trail with daisies and barley
    Down the rivers of the windfall light.

And as I was green and carefree, famous among the barns
About the happy yard and singing as the farm was home,
    In the sun that is young once only,
        Time let me play and be
    Golden in the mercy of his means,
And green and golden I was huntsman and herdsman, the calves
Sang to my horn, the foxes on the hills barked clear and cold,
        And the sabbath rang slowly
    In the pebbles of the holy streams.

All the sun long it was running, it was lovely, the hay
Fields high as the house, the tunes from the chimneys, it was air
    And playing, lovely and watery
        And fire green as grass.

And nightly under the simple stars
As I rode to sleep the owls were bearing the farm away,
All the moon long I heard, blessed among stables, the nightjars
   Flying with the ricks, and the horses
     Flashing into the dark.

And then to awake, and the farm, like a wanderer white
With the dew, come back, the cock on his shoulder: it was all
   Shining, it was Adam and maiden,
     The sky gathered again
    And the sun grew round that very day.
So it must have been after the birth of the simple light
In the first, spinning place, the spellbound horses walking warm
   Out of the whinnying green stable
     On to the fields of praise.

And honoured among foxes and pheasants by the gay house
Under the new made clouds and happy as the heart was long,
   In the sun born over and over,
     I ran my heedless ways,
    My wishes raced through the house high hay
And nothing I cared, at my sky blue trades, that time allows
In all his tuneful turning so few and such morning songs
   Before the children green and golden
     Follow him out of grace,

Nothing I cared, in the lamb white days, that time would take
  me
Up to the swallow thronged loft by the shadow of my hand,
   In the moon that is always rising,
     Nor that riding to sleep
    I should hear him fly with the high fields
And wake to the farm forever fled from the childless land.
Oh as I was young and easy in the mercy of his means,
    Time held me green and dying
   Though I sang in my chains like the sea.

          Dylan Thomas
6   (G 742)

The Fool in " Lear "

MAD as a bee or a wild shining bird,
    my only gender is to mock;
I am the sad wasp, and the robin sick
with dancing in the cold; I am the word
that opens, in your dreams, the hideous door;
I am the sex of the weather; strip me bare,
    I am the laughing-stock.

Down in the horrible mystery, the night
    and granite of the old king's mind,
the grief and writhing cracked across, went blind
and venomous: it was thence that I crept out.
Which of us, in his madness, was the man?
Only my knowledge went to bed at noon,
    his was the staring wind,

his was the bed in which I left no trace:
    nothing could prove I had been born;
I had gone back. Yet sometimes he had worn
wrinkles or troubled hair that were my face:
dying himself, it was in me he wrapped
Cordelia, one hour before I slipped
    into the cold again.

                                            Terence Tiller

Beggar

OLD as a coat on a chair; and his crushed hand,
    as unexpressive as a bird's face, held
out like an offering, symbol of the blind,
he gropes our noise for charity. You could build
his long-deserted face up out of sand,
    or bear his weakness as a child.

Shuffling the seconds of a drugged watch, he
attends no answer to his rote; for soul's
and body's terrible humility,
stripped year by year a little barer, wills
nothing: he claims no selfhood in his cry:
    his body is an age that feels.

As if a mask, a tattered blanket, should
live for a little before falling, when
the body leaves it: so briefly in his dead
feathers of rags and rags of body, and in
his crumpled mind, the awful and afraid
    stirs and pretends to be a man.

Earth's degradation and the voice of earth;
colour of earth and clothed in it; his eyes
white pebbles blind with deserts; the long growth
of landscape in his body: as if these
or these dead acres horribly gave birth:
    here will fall from him like disguise.

Only a sad and humble motion keeps
the little space he is, himself: to row
his mindless caves with ritual hand and lips,
and wonder dimly at his guilt: with no
memory of it now: it was perhaps
    too fearful, or too long ago.

Terence Tiller

Camels

I SEE them swaying their strange heads like geese,
  nineteen camels in a string like geese in flight;
as if approaching a problem, or in quest
but baffled a little, a little unsure of their right.

But I am glad their supercilious look
sees as I see the powdery town, the tall
activity of streets, the buttoned-up faces,
the cars like secret agents, the want of it all.

Gentle and sure as pianists' hands, their feet
deliberating on the stone press out
in rhythms that have nothing to do with us
the coins of their aloofness in scorn or doubt.

The motion of the blind or the very proud:
they could be blind; but where their masked eyes fall
they have the sailor's distant and innocent gaze
for where this ends, for the limit and want of it all.

Terence Tiller

A Thief to His Lord

HOLY JACK, they say your side bled gold;
  They say flame leapt from holes across your brow.
And Jack, that flowers sprouted from your hands
Where iron drove them hard against the bough.

I wish I had been there, old lad of love;
You must have looked a king upon that tree!
I'm game to wager either of my ears
The guards looked small against your majesty.

I met a woman in the tavern here
Who says they wept, the folk, to hear you jest
At being given wine upon a sponge.
And did you then? I always miss the best!

Oh! Jack, don't hold it hard against me that
I stabbed a soldier later for your coat.

Henry Treece

Lyric

OH keep your sweetness clover;
   Days will come
When men no longer wish to feast on blood.
White May, Spring's bridal daughter,
It would be shame
To lose you from the battle-shattered wood.

And lilac, loveliest as I walk
At evening time
Along the road that brings me to my home,
I know if you could talk
Your words would be fit fellows for the strain
Of virginals, and Time

Would stay his shuffling feet,
Thin hand to ear,
And listen to your poems in the hedge.
And did I forget you, sweet
Poppies, as you rear
Those gallant scarlet heads, as red as rage?

I ask forgiveness then, whose heart is small
To house all beauties that delight my soul.

Henry Treece

Flight

BY day, the returning terror of swifts, the scream
  Of the loop over leaf, the power-dive on to the thatch;
And the robin whose vivid gift is a tongue of flame
To startle the stone at your foot into lyrical speech.
By night, the approach of the bat, neurotic and odd,
A flicker of bony fingers here and there;
And the cool owl swimming in the blinded wood,
A big moth saying nothing in grey air.

By day, the shuttle of colour, speed that belongs
To the shadow that drops like a stone, the jewel that soars.
By night, the suspicion, the mere innuendo of wings,
The hint of a fugitive shadow across the stars.

By day, *Jubilate* of saints in the heart of the holly.
By night, the cry of the lost in the luminous valley.

Laurence Whistler

RETURN TO NATURALISM

POEMS OF COMMENT ON THE

CONTEMPORARY SCENE

These poets are clear-eyed and clear-headed, and they have no axe to grind. Although the style of all is simple and direct and, if you like, realistic, yet these are not poems of the head alone. The keynote of these poems is tenderness. Some are optimistic and are inspired with love and admiration for the subject; some, especially those touching on the war, are sad though not bitter. There is a great fellow-feeling about these poems—and that is the big difference between them and the poems in the previous section, which are subjective in their imagery where these look out and about on the world and humanity.

Stone Pity

SHEEP, under a wall shagged with snow,
   Hard-breathing huddle; soon the hooded crow
Shall harvest their flesh piece-meal; yon storm-sturdy stones
Holding the soft feathery surges back, shall mark the slow
Unmindful purification of their clean-picked bones,
When sweetening winds of the year's resurrection blow.

I think of men, that crawl
The length of a blocked gallery or back to wall
Stand fury-folded; aye, while shepherds grope
A frail white universe and with hoarse night lose hope.
We too, lose hurricane-proof hope.
Inwardly groan then, stones, beneath your wool-white cope!
Not for these sheep, this carrion, terrible Wall,
You stuff of me, stone pity; grieve rather for all
Creation, for love latent, summer breath
Of trapped souls under the turf, hearing the huge fall
Of coal-dust Death.

                                           Lilian Bowes Lyon

Northumbrian Farm

EARLY and very early, by a moon dawn-dimmed,
   Go clinking to the milking farmer and hind.
Hardily hands unwind
The silk-soft milk, the frothing fairy skein;
Gnomes on the lime-washed wall, for generations limned
By ritual lantern's light, we wax and wane.

Slovenly-great the old bull wakes
To his contracted kingdom, shakes
The straw from his lustreless flank in fiery flakes.
Men scatter to far fields, to the ten-acre stubble,
To the hedge-sickle and plough;
Heavily beats now
Our bull's huge heart left pondering;
                        his decadence makes
Morning come slowlier; grizzled Time in trouble.

Pastureward covetous-eyed creep
The cows again, with udders easy and slack;
Each leaves her track
Her snail's track on a world still hoar with sleep.
The half-shot-away hare
(Mark, Gentlemen of England now abed!)
Stitches a precious thread
Of blood into the upland turf—oh learning to be dead.
You see, we lose the knack.

After the black furrow (there's no turning back)
Silvery lapwing, pied plover weep
And weave a wild consolation crying Enough said,
Oh weave, child, weave a bravery through despair.
Here's speedwell too, as though the blue sky bled.

Most beauty is signed with sorrow; the iron share
Though it strike fire from flint, bites deep.

Lilian Bowes Lyon

Cleator Moor

FROM one shaft at Cleator Moor
  They mined for coal and iron ore.
This harvest below ground could show
Black and red currants on one tree.

In furnaces they burnt the coal,
The ore was smelted into steel,
And railway lines from end to end
Corseted the bulging land.

Pylons sprouted on the fells,
Stakes were driven in like nails,
And the ploughed fields of Devonshire
Were sliced with the steel of Cleator Moor.

The land waxed fat and greedy too,
It would not share the fruits it grew,
And coal and ore, as sloe and plum,
Lay black and red for jamming time.

The pylons rusted on the fells,
The gutters leaked beside the walls,
And women searched the ebb-tide tracks
For knobs of coal or broken sticks.

But now the pits are wick with men,
Digging like dogs dig for a bone:
For food and life *we* dig the earth—
In Cleator Moor they dig for death.

Every waggon of cold coal
Is fire to drive a turbine wheel;
Every knuckle of soft ore
A bullet in a soldier's ear.

The miner at the rockface stands,
With his segged and bleeding hands
Heaps on his head the fiery coal,
And feels the iron in his soul.

Norman Nicholson

Bombing Practice

IN the long estuary now the water
    At the top and turn of the tide
Is quiet as a mountain tarn,
Smooth and dull as pewter,
Pale as the mauve sea-aster
In the turf of the gutter-side.

The fells are purple and blurred in the haze above the marshes;
The gulls float like bubbles.
Plovers band together with white bellies
Square into the wind;
A curlew flies crying along the gullies;
A faint rainbow of oil is clogged in the thin rushes.

The swinging aeroplane drops seed through the air
Plumb into the water, where slowly it grows
Boles of smoke and trees
Of swelling and ballooning leafage,
Silver as willows
Or white as a blossoming pear.

The trees float seaward, spreading and filling like sails,
And the smoke mingles with the sea-mist when
The breeze shreds it. And the curlew sadly cries
That things so beautiful as these
Shall fall through nights of winter gales
And plant their germs of pain in the limbs of men.

Norman Nicholson

The Tame Hare

SHE came to him in dreams—her ears
 Diddering like antennae, and her eyes
Wide as dark flowers where the dew
Holds and dissolves a purple hoard of shadow.
The thunder clouds crouched back, and the world opened
Tiny and bright as a celandine after rain.
A gentle light was on her, so that he
Who saw the talons in the vetch
Remembered now how buttercup and daisy
Would bounce like springs when a child's foot stepped off
    them.
Oh, but never dared he touch—
Her fur was still electric to his fingers.

Yet of all the beasts blazoned in gilt and blood
In the black-bound missal of his mind,
Pentecostal dove and paschal lamb,
Eagle, lion, serpent, she alone
Lived also in the noon of ducks and sparrows;
And the cleft-mouthed kiss which plugged the night with
    fever
Was sweetened by a lunch of docks and lettuce.

                                                        Norman Nicholson

The Undiscovered Planet

OUT on the furthest tether let it run
 Its hundred-year-long orbit, cold
As solid mercury, old and dead
Before *this* world's fermenting bread
Had got a crust to cover it; landscape of lead
Whose purple voes and valleys are
Lit faintly by a sun
No nearer than a measurable star.

No man has seen it; nor the lensed eye
That pin-points week by week the same patch of sky
Records even a blur across its pupil; only
The errantry of Saturn, the wry
Retarding of Uranus, speak
Of the pull beyond the pattern:—
The unknown is shown
Only by a bend in the known.

Norman Nicholson

Movement of Bodies

THOSE of you that have got through the rest, I am going
to rapidly
Devote a little time to showing you, those that can master it,
A few ideas about tactics, which must not be confused
With what we call strategy. Tactics is merely
The mechanical movement of bodies, and that is what we
mean by it.
Or perhaps I should say: by them.

Strategy, to be quite frank, you will have no hand in.
It is done by those up above, and it merely refers to
The larger movements over which we have no control.
But tactics are also important, together or single.
You must never forget that suddenly, in an engagement,
You may find yourself alone.

This brown clay model is a characteristic terrain
Of a simple and typical kind. Its general character
Should be taken in at a glance, and its general character
You can see at a glance it is somewhat hilly by nature,
With a fair amount of typical vegetation
Disposed at certain parts.

Here at the top of the tray, which we might call the north-
        wards,
Is a wooded headland, with a crown of bushy-topped trees on;
And proceeding downwards or south we take in at a glance
A variety of gorges and knolls and plateaus and basins and
        saddles,
Somewhat symmetrically put, for easy identification.
        And here is our point of attack.

But remember of course it will not be a tray you will fight on,
Nor always by daylight. After a hot day, think of the night
Cooling the desert down, and you still moving over it:
Past a ruined tank or gun, perhaps, or a dead friend,
In the midst of war, at peace. It might quite well be that.
        It isn't always a tray.

And even this tray is different to what I had thought.
These models are somehow never always the same: for a
        reason
I do not know how to explain quite. Just as I do not know
Why there is always someone at this particular lesson
Who always starts crying. Now will you kindly
        Empty those blinking eyes?

I thank you. I have no wish to seem impatient.
I know it is all very hard, but you would not like,
To take a simple example, to take for example,
This place we have thought of here, you would not like
To find yourself face to face with it, and you not knowing
        What there might be inside?

Very well then: suppose this is what you must capture.
It will not be easy, not being very exposed,
Secluded away like it is, and somewhat protected
By a typical formation of what appear to be bushes,
So that you cannot see, as to what is concealed inside,
        As to whether it is friend or foe.

And so, a strong feint will be necessary in this connection.
It will not be a tray, remember. It may be a desert stretch
With nothing in sight, to speak of. I have no wish to be
    inconsiderate,
But I see there are two of you now, commencing to snivel.
I do not know where such emotional privates can come from.
        Try to behave like men.

I thank you. I was saying: a thoughtful deception
Is always somewhat essential in such a case. You can see
That if only the attacker can capture such an emplacement
The rest of the terrain is his: a key-position, and calling
For the most resourceful manœuvres. But that is what tactics
    is.
        Or should I say rather: are.

Let us begin then and appreciate the situation.
I am thinking especially of the point we have been considering,
Though in a sense everything in the whole of the terrain
Must be appreciated. I do not know what I have said
To upset so many of you. I know it is a difficult lesson.
        Yesterday a man was sick,

But I have never known as many as five in a single intake,
Unable to cope with this lesson. I think you had better
Fall out, all five, and sit at the back of the room,
Being careful not to talk. The rest will close up.
Perhaps it was me saying " a dead friend ", earlier on?
        Well, some of us live.

And I never know why, whenever we get to tactics,
Men either laugh or cry, though neither is strictly called for.
But perhaps I have started too early with a difficult task?
We will start again, further north, with a simpler problem.
Are you ready? Is everyone paying attention?
        Very well then. Here are two hills.

                                        Henry Reed

Guidebooks

SOME things can all be logged, like dates;
    the points of interest on the route, the best
hotels, the famous heroes with their tragic fates,
the types of landscapes and the ruined towers.
But guidebooks cannot tell you all the rest.

The real life goes on somewhere else, away
from lidos on the beach or staged, romantic ruins;
the picture postcards have their coloured say
in harbours bright with boats and sailing churches.
But life escapes them, groping in the lurch.

They do not conjure up the smells or dirt,
the children's sores who idle near the bay;
nor say that here, beneath a bloodstained shirt,
a man's heart stopped through lack of human pity.
The personal details, like indecencies, are wrapped away.

They might admit, in tones of conversation,
that these fields rotted through a lack of work,
while back at home big business crucified the nation,
and people died in half-forgotten swamps or hills
through lack of means to fight the plague that killed.

But on the printed page the words are dead,
with no more meaning than the slogans scrawled
in chalk for sold-out leaders in the village halls.
The real life went dry inside a peasant's head
who died in war to write his name upon these walls.

Alan Ross

Hiroshima

WHEN in the aftermath
    They come to stir the dust
And shards of an old myth
Will they pause before the shape
Of a prone man bitten
By the acid of the lie
Into the coffin step?
What will it mean to them
That a culture had to die
To bequeath that lightning-written
Cryptograph of stone,
That fossil shame?

O cry it across the chasm
Of ages, how we struck
In the atom's smithy a sword
That kissed with a comet's breath,
And the town conceived death
In a cyclopean orgasm.
Tell how we bent the knee
To the image of our power,
The blood-fed Upas tree
With its crown against the sky
And root clenched in the bone
Of the wronged and the wrongdoer.

Speak, lips of stone,
And make the ravished town
The bride of Sinai.

                                              Stanley Snaith

Homage to Thor Heyerdahl

YOU glorious pedant: as a professor
   Crosses a library for a book,
You saw a reference over the Pacific,
Crossed in a raft to look.

The sarcastic mainland turned away,
The seas were incredulous and loud;
Far in the west your theory lay,
Capped with a bright cloud.

A trough hung under you like an abyss:
You had been deeper than that to school
In seas of your own ignorance
And others' ridicule.

Crazy as Noah you floated on
In a world drowned fifteen centuries deep:
A south-sea Ararat came up
To admire your seamanship.

An awkward fact lay like a reef:
You drove at it, shouted hurrah.
Black and blue you broke through there,
Harder than coral far.

The beaten sea roared and lay down,
The brown girls danced, the white men waved,
Your escapade was done: says you,
" My theory is not proved ".

Here, Norwegian, take an English
Salute of guns for your seafaring.
Only so great a madman could
So re-enact the dead King's daring.
Only the already faithful find
The sandal a god was wearing.

Hal Summers

Prologue to a Theatrical Season

HERE is the place, the other country, where
    Action succeeds; even the attempted suicide
Throwing the revolver from him in disgust
Has done precisely what he ought to have done.

Where you come from, the question is always checkmate
Or the answer occurs to you when it is too late:
Here the lovers speak extempore verse
And the clown wears his wrong words like a coster's sequins.

Where you come from almost everything is irrelevant:
Here nothing is, and you can see
In the half-smile, the gesture barely discerned,
A battle wavering or a martyr burned.

Where you come from hardly anything is important:
Here everything is, even a flower, a toy,
And the falling leaf is O so light with joy
That it can scarcely fall.

So when the lights converge upon this ground,
When this shell whispers as with a sea's sound,
The play lives—yes, but where? There where you sit
Silent and dark, there breathes the being of it.

What was written centuries ago
Lives from your hand to mouth, changes with you;
The words you learned as children in class have grown
And look, their mask has sorrow in it like your own.

There's the contradiction that holds the keys
Of our whole art, its shows and mysteries,
That the country where thought is expressed and action
    succeeds
Is yours, whose mouth is twisted, whose hand bleeds.

You kill Cæsar, and Cæsar dies in you,
It is you who really laugh when the player seems to,
You ride with the explorers and you wait
Where they are expected, it is you whose hearts grow great

When from the young girl's hand flies the little white dove
And the distraught king enters the kingdom of love;
And with the departure and the last word's waste
Your lives have been rehearsed, your deaths have passed.

Hal Summers

These Are Facts

THESE are facts, observe them how you will:
   Forget for a moment the medals and the glory,
The clean shape of the bomb, designed to kill,
And the proud headlines of the paper's story.

Remember the walls of brick that forty years
Had nursed to make a neat though shabby home;
The impertinence of death, ignoring tears,
That smashed the house and left untouched the Dome.

Bodies in death are not magnificent or stately,
Bones are not elegant that blast has shattered;
This sorry, stained and crumpled rag was lately
A man whose life was made of little things that mattered;

Now he is just a nuisance, liable to stink,
A breeding-ground for flies, a test-tube for disease:
Bury him quickly and never pause to think
What is the future worth to men like these?

People are more than places, more than pride;
A million photographs record the works of Wren;
A city remains a city on credit from the tide
That flows among its rocks, a sea of men.

Ruthven Todd

It Was Easier

NOW over the map that took ten million years
Of rain and sun to crust like boiler-slag,
The lines of fighting men progress like caterpillars,
Impersonally looping between the leaf and twig.

One half the map is shaded as if by night
Or an eclipse. It is difficult from far away
To understand that a man's booted feet
May grow blistered walking there, or a boy

Die from a bullet. It is difficult to plant
That map with olives, oranges or grapes,
Or to see men alive at any given point,
To see dust-powdered faces or cracked lips.

It is easier to avoid all thought of it
And shelter in the elegant bower of legend,
To dine in dreams with kings, to float
Down the imaginary river, crowds on each hand

Cheering each mention of my favoured name.
It is easier to collect anecdotes, the tall tales
That travellers, some centuries ago, brought home,
Or wisecracks and the drolleries of fools;

It is easier to sail paper-boats on lily-ponds,
To plunge like a gannet in the sheltered sea,
To go walking or to chatter with my friends
Or to discuss the rare edition over tea,

Than to travel in the mind to that place
Where the map becomes reality, where cracks
Are gullies, a bullet more than half-an-inch
Of small newsprint and the shaped grey rocks

Are no longer the property of wandering painters,
A pleasant water colour for an academic wall,
But cover for the stoat-eyed snipers
Whose aim is fast and seldom known to fail.

It is easier . . . but no, the map has grown
And now blocks out the legends, the sweet dreams
And the chatter. The map has come alive. I hear
    the moan
Of the black planes and see their pendant bombs.

I can no longer hide in fancy: they'll hunt me out.
That map has mountains and these men have blood:
" Time has an answer!" cries my familiar ghost,
Stirred by explosives from his feather bed.

Time may have answers, but the map is here.
Now is the future that I never wished to see.
I was quite happy dreaming and had no fear:
But now, from the map, a gun is aimed at me.

                                                    Ruthven Todd

Docks

WHEN paint or steel or wood are wearing thin,
  Then they come in:
The liners, schooners, merchantmen and tramps,
Upon a head of water pressing hard
On gates of greenheart wood, that close and guard
The docks, till lintels, clamps,
Swing suddenly on quoins steel-pivoted,
With harsh complaint and clang,
And then above the walls arise and spread
Top-gallant yards or funnel, spanker-vang
Or dolphin-striker; figure-heads arise,
That settling sway
Beside an inn; a mermaid's breasts and eyes
Beneath a bowsprit glare beside a dray.

All docks are wonderful, whether beside
The estuaries or foreshores robbed of sea,
Where jetties and much dredging keep them free,
And the strong constant scouring of the tide
Sweeps down the silt; or where by sandy dune
The neap-tides leave them dry, or flood-tides dash
With a vindictive lash
At the conjunction of the sun and moon.
And wonderful are dry docks, where the ships
Are run on keel-props held by timber-shores,
And sterns and prores
Stand up for scrapers' work, and the paint drips
Among algae and mussels; wonderful when
Docks still are in the building, and the pumps
Move water from the sumps,
And derricks, little trains, and shouting men
Dump clustered cylinders upon the gravel,
And through the sky square blocks of granite travel,
Dangling to place to make the sills. Or when

As now by Thames the running currents flush
The sluices of the locks, and seek to rush
Reverse-gates strengthening the entrances,
Harry the boats, and shift
The refuse of the town and littoral drift;
And in the dusk the slums are palaces.

They wait upon the sea,
And wharf and jetty, stately in the grime,
Make commerce classical, and turn sublime
The warehouse crammed with jute, or flax or tea.

Dorothy Wellesley

The Traffic Problem in East Anglia

SO pass the ribbon first and make a name!
For aimless speed's itself sufficient aim!
Come, speed the engines up! Betting's begun!
Vibrations will wreck abbeys ere you've done,
Windows of Crowland, where in place of glass
Are framed the coloured dawns, and sea birds pass
Easily in and over the altars bare.
Then shatter the village fane,
And barefoot roads of pilgrims! Speed again!
Shake the pale shrines on marshes of the seas
No longer built with hands
But kept by memories
That serve like moving light of priests the altars of these lands:
The inmost jewels, sweet waxes tapering true,
The shrine at Walsingham Erasmus knew.

Dorothy Wellesley

Back to the House

IN dusk when the dead heart rejoices,
   In dusk when the bittern calls,
Over sheeted slopes come the voices
Of the lost waterfalls.

Together they cry as in old days:
Rocky steps on the hilly steep,
So I have heard them in old days,
In the cot asleep.

I will go up those stairs
Barefoot by the waterfalls again,
Step by step and by stones to the lost house,
Where once dwelt women and men.

I will climb those stony stairs
Like a holy man on his knees;
Going with moths, and eternal music
Made by water under the trees.

I will climb the falls from the long lake
Where the bittern and badger cry,
For the birds and the beasts and the dead
Pretty fellows,
Are my friends before I die.

Dorothy Wellesley

REBIRTH OF SIMPLE LYRICISM

POEMS OF LOVE HOPE, AND FAITH

At the end of the fifty-year cycle, we find once more simple poetry of feeling: here are poems of grief and loss, of pity, delight in Nature and in beauty, and a passionate longing for the solace of religion. Included among the younger poets are three persistent Romantics, who throughout half a century of industrial and scientific progress and the double cataclysm of war, have kept alive their lyrical gift and simplicity of vision. These are, Edmund Blunden with his love for the little things in nature, John Masefield, the Poet Laureate and worshipper of Beauty, and Walter de la Mare, who has never lost the magical essence and enchanting melody which make him one of our greatest poets.

The Summer Dove

THERE was dazzling sunlight on the day of my friend's funeral,
And the parson's surplice bellied like a sail in the summer wind.
I remember thinking: What a heavenly day for a burial—
As I heard about beauty like a moth-fretted garment,
About grass, and flowers, and fleeing shadows,
The glory of the sun, and immortality.
Beautiful words I caught at the funeral service of my friend,
Fragment of a sentence here, and there another fragment,
In the summer wind tossed so lightly
And sent far adrift like thistledown over the shining meadows.

But I wanted to laugh with my friend at the absurdity
Of all that dire solemnity
Where the black-rook mourners and the magpie parson
    gathered near the hole in the ground!
Whilst a lizard panted on the wall near-by,
And I caught an interested robin's bold appraising eye.
Then I grew drowsy with a dove's perpetual, soothing, cool
    and leafy sound.

Walking home by the field-path after my friend's funeral,
Aware of the indefinable singing of the summer day,
I thought: Well, everything goes on as usual,
After all the dead can never be so important
As the living; it is Life that is warm and urgent,
And Death certainly can claim no victory
For where's victory when whatever you touch simply crumbles
    away?
And for crumbling, what so appropriate as a hole in the
    ground? . . .
Then I grew drowsy with a dove's perpetual, soothing, cool
    and leafy sound.

Since that was how things happened yesterday
It seems strange that to-day
Hearing the cool-voiced dove I am suddenly blind in my
    pain,
Blind and wrung with the piercing of my sorrow. . . .
And I must hear, oh I must hear the summer dove again
To-morrow, and to-morrow. . . .

Frances Bellerby

Genesis

NOW from the dark soul of that profound sea
    A cry comes, with no words, no form.
Must then the Sun translate? Can only the Stars perceive
Shape, truth, in the chaos? The Lord
Of Life in His rapturous agony? Twin power,
Of Love in the root, of Death in the deathless flower?

I will lay down my darling, life, at the feet of Life
Can I but share the Sun's wisdom,
Can I but share the vision, unblunted by sight,
Of the piercing Stars—The kingdom
Is ready, is ready, O hesitant glorious King!—
Time, for your restless grief; Space, for your soaring.

I will bury my heart, for love, at the cross-roads here;
Myself plunge the stake—that priceless sword
Which no outcast, no pauper, lacks. Myself, without fear,
Lift up these eyes to the hills. Flaming Word!
Slash them to blindness that I for one instant may see
As the Sun, the Stars, as God in His agony!

Frances Bellerby

Two Small Elegies

(i) *The Hedgehog killed on the Road*

UNSPEEDY friend, poor earth-child, whose sad eyes
   Seemed, when I met you creeping past in life,
To expect no luck from giants of other spheres,
I mourn you lying here; and in your shape
Coiled with vain skill for the last time, in your quills
Slackened and puny, see too deep resemblance
To other troubles, other reasonless
Downbursts of death, beyond your now dead brain,
And yet much like your own. Earth-child, these tears.

(ii) *The Snail*

UNDER the bus wheel comes the tiny snail
   With all the touch of exquisite accord
Which drew it through the showery world, with all
The accomplished painting of that rounded shard.
A child's eye drooped, so gleamed the ring-bright shell,
And then the time was up, the thing occurred:
Softly the huge car stopped, with wheel as still
As that slain mystery, hardly discernible.

Edmund Blunden

After the Bombing

MY hesitant design it was, in a time when no man feared,
   To make a poem on the last poor flower to have grown
   on the patch of land
Where since a gray enormous stack of shops and offices reared
Its bulk as though to eternity there to stand.

Moreover I dreamed of a lyrical verse to welcome another
flower,
The first to blow on that hidden site when the concrete block
should cease
Gorging the space; it could not be mine to foretell the means,
the hour,
But nature whispered something of a longer lease.

We look from the street now over a breezy wilderness of
bloom,
Now, crowding its colours between the sills and cellars, hosts
of flame
And foam, pearl-pink and thunder-red, befriending the make-
shift tomb
Of a most ingenious but impermanent claim.

Edmund Blunden

Listen!

QUIET your faces; be crossed every thumb;
   Fix on me deep your eyes . . .
Out of my mind a story shall come,
   Old, and lovely, and wise.

Old as the pebbles that fringe the cold seas;
   Lovely as apples in rain;
Wise as the King who learned of the bees,
   Then learned of the emmets again.

Old as the fruits that in mistletoe shine;
   Lovely as amber, as snow;
Wise as the fool who, when care made him pine,
   Sang hey, fol lol, lilly lo!

Old as the woods rhyming Thomas snuffed sweet,
   When pillion he rid with the Queen;
Lovely as elf-craft; wise as the street,
   Where the roofs of the humble are seen. . . .

Hsst! there's a stirring, there's wind in the bough;
   A whirring of birds on the wing:
Like a river of water my story shall flow,
   Like runnels of water sing.

Walter de la Mare

But, Oh, My Dear

HEARTS that too wildly beat—
   Brief is their epitaph!
Wisdom is in the wheat,
   Not in the chaff.
But, Oh, my dear, how rich and rare, and root-down-deep
and wild and sweet
   It is to laugh!

Walter de la Mare

And So to Bed

"NIGHT - NIGHT, my Precious!"; "*Sweet* dreams,
   Sweet!"
"Heaven bless you, Child!"—the accustomed grown-ups
   said.
Two eyes gazed mutely back that none could meet,
Then turned to face Night's terrors overhead.

Walter de la Mare

An Island

PARCHED, panting, he awoke; phantasmal light
Blueing the hollows of his fevered eyes;
And strove to tell of what he had dreamed that night—
In stumbling words its meaning to devise:

An island, lit with beauty, like a flower
Its sea of sapphire fringed with ocean's snow,
Whose music and beauty with the changing hour
Seemed from some inward source to ebb and flow;
A heart, all innocence and innately wise,
Well-spring of very love appeared to be—
" A candle whose flame," he stammered, " never dies,
But feeds on light itself perpetually.
Me! This! A thing corrupt on the grave's cold brink,
And into outer darkness soon to sink!"

The tired nurse yawned. " A queer dream that!" she said.
" But now you are awake. And see, it's day."
She smoothed the pillow for his sweat-dark head,
Smiled, frowned " There, sleep again!" and turned away.

Walter de la Mare

Time and the Ocean

I HAD been time and the ocean away:
Absence was bitter, a desert without love.
My fears, like rust, had crumbled half away
Places the eye cherished with its persistent love.
What I thought of was the autumn happy orchards desolate,
The copse by the stream cut, so water gave back empty sky;
The raven cold and dusty without his mate:
And my friend's life done and I would not be by.

8   (G 742)

When I returned the changes were not these.
Only my own thoughts had laid waste the ground.
There were no failing waters, no cut trees;
Boughs only bent more closely to the ground
Their wavering fires of fruit. Haycocks and corn
Let their pale clouds of light fall on earth gently.
Yet the men coming from the fields were sober and worn
And the faces of the aged were aged more bitterly.

" It seems like yesterday you left ", one told me briefly.
But the day I left still shook me with its grief; and alone
At the other end of what seemed infinity,
I knew this homecoming cold as rain on stone.

Kenneth Gee

Delight in Water

BEAUTY of water gave delight again:—
The earth was shining after winter rain,
Each little brook was shouting in its run
Each meadow was a jewel in the sun,
And in a midmost grass a foot-high fount
Throbbed and uptumbled its collapsing mount
Wonder, dissolved, resolved, upspringing, sped,
Beauty, yet never aught, yet never dead.

Terror of water followed, when I saw
The eddies of a flood in torrent draw
The wreckage under, as though hands were there
Hands, and the will to make a boy beware.
Even in summer when the pools were clear
The quiet depth was brooded-on by fear,
To be within its power was to die,
For all its still, reflected earth and sky.

But exquisite delight my spirit took
In many a roadside—many a meadow-brook,
One above all so beautiful a thing
I thought God had a cottage at its spring.
And by another once a partridge came
With chicks which I could stroke, they were so tame
Quick, pecking, peering, all the mottled clutch
Bright-eyed, unfearing, exquisite to touch.

One other water blessed me with her grace,
A deep, calm quiet in a sunny place,
Where yellow flags grew tall and reeds grew gray
As though all time would be a summer day.
Sometimes a ring would spread as a fish rose
Then, the ring spent, placidity would close,
A skating fly might skim, a shadow flit
As some exulting swallow stooped at it,
But save for these, no other aim there was
Than to be beauty and beauty's looking-glass.

John Masefield

February Night

I WENT into the land where Beauty dwells.
The winter darkness shut it as a prison.
The thin moon, due at midnight, had not risen.
The clouds moved slowly over: nothing else
Stirred, nor did owl cry, nor did glow-worm glisten.
The night in all her vastness stood to listen.
Then in the valley church, men rang the bells.

Out of the tower into the winter air
They shook their triumph: and a hill beyond
Made laggard ghosts of echoes to respond.
As turbulent water beats the boulder bare
And hurries and leaps, so turbulent drin and drone
Clanged and were spilled in cataracts of tone
Out of the tower above the ringers there.

Then the bells ceased; the men, as I suppose
Muffling their throats in woollens, trudged to bed.
The Heaven displayed her star-work overhead
Star beyond star, the brighter as it froze.
A fox barked thrice, none answered, the world slept,
Save at some oven where a cricket kept
Trilling the drowsy cat into a doze.

John Masefield

Lapwings in March

DO not make my grave the time I die
      Anywhere near lapwings, not where the lapwings fly
With clamorous assault upon the sky;
For sure as there's a night and day
However long my sleep, however deep I lie
I will rise up if I should hear that cry
Like Gabriel's trump a summons to obey;
I will rise up, as there is day and night,
To see their wind-begotten flight,
A throwing up and down of black and white
Like often eclipsed stars;
I will rise up and haunt that place,
I, death in the midst of life, without the bars
Of time, the frame of space.

Averil Morley

The Baby

IT never saw the sun
  For it was born at night
By pale candle light
And died before the morning was begun.

No wind, no bird,
No other sound it heard
But the nurse sighing
When she saw it was dying.

What God and man have made,
What was ten million decades growing
In time's vast cavalcade,
It held for an hour without knowing.

Averil Morley

Fair is the Water

FAIR is the water when the land is fainting,
  fair on the braided tresses of the barley:
fair as it falls from heaven to the rose, and
        lies in its bosom:

fair is the water when the wind is urging
waves against land as horse against a city:
the wave-form at the crest of motion peerless,
        fair in its falling.

Fairest is water when the heart at evening
leads the fond feet to the familiar places:
fairest is water when it falls in silent
        dew where thou liest.

Ruth Pitter

Thanksgiving For a Fair Summer

NOW, before the wheat
    Standing so nobly, falls:
Ere yet the first owl calls,
Or that thin sickle and fleet
Of harvest moon her earliest quarter passes,
Or the ground-frost may crisp the twice-mown grasses:
Now let me sing
My quiet stave, when redbreast too
Sings in, as I beneath, the yew:
Before they bring
The apples home, and once again
The equinox beats down the leaves in rain.

We had thought summer dead:
Year upon year
Prone in the furrow lay the smutted ear;
More wan than red
Hung tasteless fruit; flowers made earth their bier:
Kine to the lowering sky
Frowned in mute patience, and the hooded hind
Driving them home, in the soft ruts plodded by
With streaming shoulders and a heart unkind,
Sullen and bowed
Against a swagging heap of swollen cloud.

But now hot camomile in headlands grows,
Coarse-smelling as from toil of reaping; bees
Their delicate harvest in the rusty rows
Of scarlet bean, and woodbine that still blows,
Though flower with berry, gather and do not cease:
No mushroom yet, for dryness of the leas:
No leaf too early sere, for droughty root,
Drops from the trees,
But grave broad green guards the thick purple fruit.

Not only thanks for ample grain,
And apple that shall give her wine
As in old seasons, strong again;
Not for low streams where lilies shine
In many a pool unvexed by flood,
Unvexed by aught but boys at play:
Not only for the sun in the blood
And the long, blest, eventless day;

But chiefly for the sign,
For the fair time as token of grace
That life is yet benign,
That this our race
Still doth possess a pleasant place:
For many a doubt
Assails us, and might overthrow,
Were not the bow
Of blessing high in heaven hung out;
Our time is dark,
And save such miracle as this
Where is the mark
To steer by, in our bitter mysteries?

Ruth Pitter

So I Praise These

D O not suppose
    The amazing daffodil has thrust
From the waste plot
Or the polluted dust.

Nor was the soil
From which a gallantry of roses flowered,
Luckless, unhusbanded,
By God or mankind soured.

So I praise these,
The gallant, the amazing, who from chance
Of birth or circumstance
This darker hour enhance.

In praising them
I celebrate a soil which is still sweet
In mine and mill,
In meadow and in street.

John Pudney

Prayer

OPEN the gates of sky to me, open the gate
     Not into my death, but out of me, into that peace
Where sun and moon revolve; whose light beats
Upon the upturned face of every day
Of partial beauty, partial love, partial pity.

Open the arms of life to me, name me, claim me
Bride me, hide me, on a mountain lay me, on a cloud
While the womb spins dreams, and the stars' spindles
Turn, and the forests and birds are woven
Into the distance of the heart's separation.

Or teach me, flower or angel, how with compassion
In time, in pain, this humble joy of living
May be the golden sowing of heaven's harvest,
The texture of a song, the exaltation
Of Christ most high, whose love is greatest.

Kathleen Raine

The Rose

WHAT does the eye see?
A rose-bud on a paradise tree.

What does hope say?
A rose shall fill time with eternity!

What is memory's refrain?
" I was that rose before the world began."

What does thought foretell?
Petal upon petal,
World within world, star within cell.

What sings love then?
" I am the rose, that crimson rose is mine."

Why comes death this way?
To take away, to take my rose away.

What lies in the immortal centre hidden?
Mary on the golden throne of heaven.

And in the heart of Heaven what lives, what grows?
The heart of Heaven is the rose, the rose!

Kathleen Raine

Ecce Homo

THOSE eyes that opened on our earth at Bethlehem
    Were all the world's young eyes; the eyes of birds,
Wild creatures' eyes that know earth's secret places,
The bee's hexagonal vision of bright flowers,
And the first delicate flagellate touched by the sun
When hope first kindled sense to live and rise;
Our childhood's innocent eyes, all human eyes
That weep and wonder, watch, and suffer and surmise.

His feet that trod the road to Calvary
Travelled the long distance of the human way
Of the fruit-gathering nomads who, wearied out, died
    where they lay;
Trod the long dance to death through man's first villages
Whose lean dead chiefs hang withered in the trees;
The steps of workmen carrying hods of clay,
Of country men trudging the long mile home,
The streets of cities where feet pass all day,
And the long road that soldiers march away.

His long thoughts, from eternity to eternity
Took on with human form the human past,
The astral pattern, matter's forms and laws,
Man's free-will, the discontinuous electron,
The slow growth and the sleep of the green tree,
The instinct and the impulse of the nerve,
And narrow prison of the skeleton;
All time, all being, the incarnate memory
Chose, in a world of chance, the identity of God.

And on the holy cross, by Him outpoured
The life-stream of entire creation flowed
Down from those veins whose life flows in us all;
And every heartbeat of the world shed from His side
Blood of the dying deer, the wounded bird,
The slain archaic king, workman, and murderer,
Those who die unfulfilled, and in despair,
The young forgotten soldier choked with sand,
All those who go down in that soundless sea
With all the human mystery in its tide
That washes for ever the long shores of the world.

Kathleen Raine

For this Time

NOW that the firmament on high,
Noah's peace-promising sky,
Is given over to an enemy,
And that those durable lights the stars
Fuse and explode, and friendly fires
Are travestied in the bomb's brightness,
And homes made hostile as the darkness;
Now country people look towards town,
And awestruck see the crimson stain
Spread on the cloud, and *London's burning*
Say in grief as once laughing:
From such a conflict, fire and frenzy,
Where should we turn unless Lord to Thee?
That Thou wouldst teach us to bear calmly
The invisible battles overhead,
And to get us through the night without dread.
Teach us therefore so to live
That we may fear our noisy bed
As little as our more peaceful grave.

Anne Ridler

Cornish Landscape

THE rich red of evening sun on the harrowed field,
    The chittering of birds,
The insistent drone of planes out at sea,
The scolding rooks,
The colder tones of the water:
What is there in a Cornish hedge,
The broken herring-bone pattern of stones,
The gorse, the ragged rick,
The way the little elms are,
Sea-bent, sea-shorn,
That so affects the heart?

A. L. Rowse

A Blue Day

ON the clouded flaxen beaches
    And on the moonstone-coloured stretches
Where the tide ebbs or streams are spread
Fanning to sea, the sky has laid
A wing of blue; on all that lies,
Water and land, between these eyes
And the indiscernible vanishing,
Has laid the one butterfly wing.

Ribbon-streams of lighter blue,
Veining of wing or leaf, lead through
To a mirage of lagoons and coast
In the sulphur-touched, the scabious mist;
Here sheaves of ragwort rust to brown
From gold on stalk where the cliff runs down.
All else, the papery grass-blades even
Are stained with blue by the gaze of heaven.

E. J. Scovell

The Giraffe

FOR neck, a tulip-stalk;
   Flower-head, far off and elegant;
Tongue, to fill your body's want
Stretched out like hands of a lady
Who takes her own naturally;
Wind netted in your small-paced walk;

Eyes dark and innocent;
Airy beast with flower's grace,
With bird's speed, with human face;
Painted like ground under trees
With light and shade; supple as these;
Horizon's instrument:

Strength flowers, speed, in you.
Speed is your soul's obedience.
Tiger and strolling wolf must dance
To other tunes, obeying God.
Strength is their fruit, who feed on blood;
But the trees kneel for you.

O meshed among high leaves,
Among clouds: I should never start
To see, when clouds or branches part,
Like a wild cherub's, bloom your head,
Serpent wise, dove feathers spread
Brushing the poplar's sleeves.

                                        E. J. Scovell

Longtailed Tit

ALL the spinney is active with chur and bat-squeak,
     with flutter, flit, dip, dropping buoyant of bodies through
     the air,
jostling of cones, twig springing, twirling to ground of needles,
as tits and goldcrests swing and hustle in the bunchy trees.

Busy the goldcrest, high squeaking, under the needly
green fall of leaf forgetting the North Sea,
in inches of light whole-hearted, a spot of spirit.

The longtail lunging and lingering through the air,
a mouse, rush-tail, a ball, wool-feather, peeper,
looking so sharp through cherry blankets of down,
the doll-face, easy on the flying twig's trapeze,
pink and white in the light, as light as blowing seed,
is meek in merriment, all careless of air's bitterness,
the bare-tooth coming, bark-biting of the winter wind.

                                                    Rex Warner

Poem

WHAT I watch most is moss
     or leaves in alleys of air,
the rasping blade of grass,
tiny berries on a huge moor;

the sparkling black bill
of stonechat on a spine,
water tumbling from a pool,
or a hawk in the sky alone.

But what most moves my mind
is torture of man by man;
how hearts in every land
are stamped upon like stone;

how ceremony cheats,
and how the law defrauds,
reason gives false weights,
and goodness goes by moods;

how love is made to lose,
and those who are high hate;
how truth is taught to please,
and freshness finds defeat.

The bright eye, the sure
mind, the bearing flesh,
what sees the future clear
is made to feel the lash.

Then we who sit on a cliff
and stare across the sea,
listening to the clanging laugh
of gulls, the curlew's cry,

who look through lanes of green,
and bask in summer peace,
must see in the iron rain
our beauty ablaze.

Rex Warner

Ophelia

STUNNED in the stone light, laid among the lilies,
Still in the green wave, graven in the reed-bed.
Lip-read by clouds in the language of the shallows,
Lie there, reflected.

Soft come the eddies, cold between your fingers.
Rippling through cresses, willow-trunk and reed-root,
Gropes the grey water; there the resting mayfly
Burns like an emerald.

Haunting the path, Laertes falls to Hamlet;
He, the young Dane, the mover of your mountains,
Sees the locked lids, your nunnery of sorrows,
Drowned in oblivion.

Silvered with dawn, the pattern of the bridge-vault
Dancing, a light-skein woven by the stream there,
Travels through shade the story of your dying,
Sweet-named Ophelia.

Dense was your last night, thick with stars unnumbered.
Bruised, the reeds parted. Under them the mud slipped,
Yielding. Scuttling and terrified, the moorhen
Left you to sink there.

Few, faint the petals carried on the surface,
Watched by those bright eyes ambushed under shadow,
Mouse, bird and insect, bore you witness, keeping
Pace ever silent.

Here, then, you lingered, late upon the world's rim,
Matched here the prince-like, stopped, and were con-
        founded,
Finding that image altered in the water's
Bitter remembrance.

Passion recalls the tumult of your story,
Midnight revives it, where your name is printed;
Yet from the water, intimate, there echoes:
" Tell this to no man ".

Bride-veils of mist fall, brilliant are the sunbeams,
Open the great leaves, all the birds are singing.
Still unawake in purity of darkness
Whiter than daylight

Dream the soft lids, the white, the deathly sleeping;
Closed are the lashes: day is there a legend.
Rise from the fair flesh, from the midnight water,
Child too soon buried.

                                                    Vernon Watkins

Wind and Rain

A MISCHIEVOUS gardener took
    An axe, and swung it low;
Then the jasmine shook
And earth and root forsook,
Severed at a blow.

A stump is all
That wood of stars is now;
Yet this hanging bough,
Fastened by a hook,
Takes life from a bare wall.

Who can explain despair?
Rootless, unstable
To the eye of care,
It yet has lived,
Finding a root in air.

Let the Judgment drift
With Moses' table,
With swallow and swift,
Down a slanting beam;
The end is supreme:

Life is a gift.

What miracle, this tree
With swallows thrown
In rootless ecstasy
Exiled from earth, alone
With air and stone!

Finches alighting there
Swing, but do not fall.
Diving, they dare
To preen their wings and call,
Held by a thread in air.

9

Thought sentenced those young leaves
That face the driving West
To die from eaves
That hide a feathered nest;
Yet thought deceives.

There grafted, all is stable,
The starlike, chaliced light
From midnight's gable
Falling in blossoms white.
Learn from this fable:

Stronger the seed than pain
Though shock and violence rive,
Black life will shoot again
And quickly will revive
If it have wind and rain.

Vernon Watkins

Good Friday in War

THE quickening woods a springtime theme unfold
    Where pale the celandines their sunlight spill;
Yet who can count the limbs which in this mould
    Feed the wild daffodil?

While birch and hawthorn spurt new flame of green,
From the great world-heart echoes such a sigh
As on that Friday, when the Nazarene
    Bowed his dark head to die.

Margaret Willy

ROMANTIC AND INTELLECTUAL

TWO GREAT POETS

Both these poets, so different in temperament, are awake to the spiritual needs of mankind: Edith Sitwell deeply involved in man's tragedy, condemns his outrage upon the living body of Christ, which is his fellow-man, and prophesies the wrath to come if expiation is not made; and T. S. Eliot, intellectual-realist, satirist, deeply concerned with the meaning and function of words, searches, with almost mystical intensity, after spiritual truth.

Still Falls the Rain

The Raids, 1940. *Night and Dawn.*

STILL falls the Rain—
    Dark as the world of man, black as our loss—
Blind as the nineteen hundred and forty nails
Upon the Cross.

Still falls the Rain
With a sound like the pulse of the heart that is changed to the
        hammer-beat
In the Potter's Field, and the sound of the impious feet

On the Tomb:
                    Still falls the Rain
In the Field of Blood where the small hopes breed and the
        human brain
Nurtures its greed, that worm with the brow of Cain.

Still falls the Rain
At the feet of the Starved Man hung upon the Cross.
Christ that each day, each night, nails there, have mercy on
        us—
On Dives and on Lazarus:
Under the Rain the sore and the gold are as one.

Still falls the Rain—
Still falls the Blood from the Starved Man's wounded Side:
He bears in His Heart all wounds—those of the light that
        died,

The last faint spark
In the self-murdered heart, the wounds of the sad uncom-
  prehending dark,
The wounds of the baited bear—
The blind and weeping bear whom the keepers beat
On his helpless flesh . . . the tears of the hunted hare.

Still falls the Rain—
Then—O Ile leape up to my God: who pulles me doune—
See, see where Christ's blood streames in the firmament:
It flows from the Brow we nailed upon the tree
Deep to the dying, to the thirsting heart
That holds the fires of the world—dark-smirched with pain
As Cæsar's laurel crown.

Then sounds the voice of One who like the heart of man
Was once a child who among beasts has lain—
" Still do I love, still shed my innocent light, my Blood, for
  thee."

Edith Sitwell

Dirge for the New Sunrise

*(Fifteen minutes past eight o'clock, on the morning of Monday the
6th of August, 1945)*

BOUND to my heart as Ixion to the wheel,
  Nailed to my heart as the Thief upon the Cross,
I hang between our Christ and the gap where the world was
  lost

And watch the phantom Sun in Famine Street
—The ghost of the heart of Man . . . red Cain
And the more murderous brain
Of Man, still redder Nero that conceived the death
Of his mother Earth, and tore
Her womb, to know the place where he was conceived.

But no eyes grieved—
For none were left for tears:
They were blinded as the years
Since Christ was born. Mother or Murderer, you have given
    or taken life—
Now all is one!

There was a morning when the holy Light
Was young. The beautiful First Creature came
To our water-springs, and thought us without blame.

Our hearts seemed safe in our breasts and sang to the Light—
The marrow in the bone
We dreamed was safe . . . the blood in the veins, the sap in
    the tree
Were springs of Deity.

But I saw the little Ant-men as they ran
Carrying the world's weight of the world's filth
And the filth in the heart of Man—
Compressed till those lusts and greeds had a greater heat than
    that of the Sun.

And the ray from that heat came soundless, shook the sky
As if in search of food, and squeezed the stems
Of all that grows on earth till they were dry
—And drank the marrow of the bone:
The eyes that saw, the lips that kissed, are gone
Or black as thunder lie and grin at the murdered Sun.

The living blind and seeing Dead together lie
As if in love. . . . There was no more hating then,
And no more love: Gone is the heart of Man.

Edith Sitwell

From: *The Shadow of Cain*

.   .   .   .

THE thunders of the Spring began. . . . We came again
    After that long migration
To the city built before the Flood by our brother Cain.

And when we reached an open door
The Fate said " My feet ache."
The Wanderers said " Our hearts ache."

There was great lightning
In flashes coming to us over the floor:
The Whiteness of the Bread
The Whiteness of the Dead
The Whiteness of the Claw—
All this coming to us in flashes through the open door.

There were great emerald thunders in the air
In the violent Spring, the thunders of the sap and the blood
    in the heart
—The Spiritual Light, the physical Revelation.

In the streets of the City of Cain there were great Rainbows
Of emeralds: the young people, crossing and meeting.

And everywhere
The great voice of the Sun in sap and bud
Fed from the heart of Being, the panic Power,
The sacred Fury, shouts of Eternity
To the blind eyes, the heat in the winged seed, the fire in the
    blood

And through the works of Death,
The dust's aridity, is heard the sound
Of mounting saps like monstrous bull-voices of unseen fear-
    ful mimes:
And the great rolling world-wide thunders of that drumming
    underground

Proclaim our Christ, and roar " Let there be harvest!
Let there be no more Poor—
For the Son of God is sowed in every furrow!"

We did not heed the Cloud in the Heavens shaped like the
    hand
Of Man. . . . But there came a roar as if the Sun and Earth
    had come together—
The Sun descending and the Earth ascending
To take its place above . . . the Primal Matter
Was broken, the womb from which all life began,
Then to the murdered Sun a totem pole of dust arose in
    memory of Man.

        .   .   .   .

There are no thunders, there are no fires, no suns, no earth-
    quakes
Left in our blood. . . . But yet like the rolling thunders of all
    the fires in the world, we cry
To Dives: " You are the shadow of Cain. Your shade is the
    primal Hunger."
" I lie under what condemnation?"
" The same as Adam, the same as Cain, the same as Sodom,
    the same as Judas."

And the fires of your Hell shall not be quenched by the rain
From those torn and parti-coloured garments of Christ, those
    rags
That once were Men. Each wound, each stripe,
Cries out more loudly than the voice of Cain—

Saying " Am I my brother's keeper?" Think! When the
    last clamour of the Bought and Sold
The agony of Gold
Is hushed. . . . When the last Judas-kiss
Has died upon the cheek of the Starved Man Christ, these
    ashes that were Men

Will rise again
To be our Fires upon the Judgment Day,
And yet—who dreamed that Christ has died in vain?
He walks again on the Seas of Blood, He comes in the terrible
    Rain.

Edith Sitwell

From: The Rock

.   .   .   .

I JOURNEYED to London, to the timekept City,
  Where the River flows, with foreign flotations.
There I was told: we have too many churches,
And too few chop-houses. There I was told:
Let the vicars retire. Men do not need the Church
In the place where they work, but where they spend their
    Sundays.
In the City, we need no bells:
Let them waken the suburbs.
I journeyed to the suburbs, and there I was told:
We toil for six days, on the seventh we must motor
To Hindhead, or Maidenhead.
If the weather is foul we stay at home and read the papers.
In industrial districts, there I was told
Of economic laws.
In the pleasant countryside, there it seemed
That the country now is only fit for picnics.
And the Church does not seem to be wanted
In country or in suburb; and in the town
Only for important weddings.

.   .   .   .

The world turns and the world changes,
But one thing does not change.
In all of my years, one thing does not change.
However you disguise it, this thing does not change:
The perpetual struggle of Good and Evil.

Forgetful, you neglect your shrines and churches;
The men you are in these times deride
What has been done of good, you find explanations
To satisfy the rational and enlightened mind.
Second, you neglect and belittle the desert.
The desert is not remote in southern tropics,
The desert is not only around the corner,
The desert is squeezed in the tube-train next to you,
The desert is in the heart of your brother.

What life have you if you have not life together?
There is no life that is not in community,
And no community not lived in praise of GOD.
Even the anchorite who meditates alone,
For whom the days and nights repeat the praise of GOD,
Prays for the Church, the Body of Christ incarnate.
And now you live dispersed on ribbon roads,
And no man knows or cares who is his neighbour
Unless his neighbour makes too much disturbance,
But all dash to and fro in motor cars,
Familiar with the roads and settled nowhere.
Nor does the family even move about together,
But every son would have his motor cycle,
And daughters ride away on casual pillions.

O weariness of men who turn from GOD
To the grandeur of your mind and the glory of your action,
To arts and inventions and daring enterprises,
To schemes of human greatness thoroughly discredited,
Binding the earth and the water to your service,
Exploiting the seas and developing the mountains,
Dividing the stars into common and preferred,
Engaged in devising the perfect refrigerator,
Engaged in working out a rational morality,
Engaged in printing as many books as possible,
Plotting of happiness and flinging empty bottles,
Turning from your vacancy to fevered enthusiasm
For nation or race or what you call humanity;

Though you forget the way to the Temple,
There is one who remembers the way to your door:
Life you may evade, but Death you shall not.
You shall not deny the Stranger.

T. S. Eliot

A Song for Simeon

LORD, the Roman hyacinths are blooming in bowls and
   The winter sun creeps by the snow hills;
The stubborn season has made stand.
My life is light, waiting for the death wind,
Like a feather on the back of my hand.
Dust in sunlight and memory in corners
Wait for the wind that chills towards the dead land.

Grant us thy peace.
I have walked many years in this city,
Kept faith and fast, provided for the poor,
Have given and taken honour and ease.
There went never any rejected from my door.
Who shall remember my house, where shall live my children's
   children
When the time of sorrow is come?
They will take to the goat's path, and the fox's home,
Fleeing from the foreign faces and the foreign swords.

Before the time of cords and scourges and lamentation
Grant us thy peace.
Before the stations of the mountain of desolation,
Before the certain hour of maternal sorrow,
Now at this birth season of decease,
Let the Infant, the still unspeaking and unspoken Word,
Grant Israel's consolation
To one who has eighty years and no to-morrow.

According to thy word.
They shall praise Thee and suffer in every generation
With glory and derision,
Light upon light, mounting the saints' stair.
Not for me the martyrdom, the ecstasy of thought and prayer,
Not for me the ultimate vision.
Grant me thy peace.
(And a sword shall pierce thy heart,
Thine also.)
I am tired with my own life and the lives of those after me,
I am dying in my own death and the deaths of those after me.
Let thy servant depart,
Having seen thy salvation.

T. S. Eliot

The Dry Salvages

I

I DO not know much about gods; but I think that the
    river
Is a strong brown god—sullen, untamed and intractable,
Patient to some degree, at first recognized as a frontier;
Useful, untrustworthy, as a conveyor of commerce;
Then only a problem confronting the builder of bridges.
The problem once solved, the brown god is almost forgotten
By dwellers in cities—ever, however, implacable,
Keeping his seasons and rages, destroyer, reminder
Of what men choose to forget. Unhonoured, unpropitiated
By worshippers of the machine, but waiting, watching and
    waiting.
His rhythm was present in the nursery bedroom.
In the rank ailanthus of the April dooryard,
In the smell of grapes on the autumn table,
And the evening circle in the winter gaslight.

The river is within us, the sea is all about us;
The sea is the land's edge also, the granite
Into which it reaches, the beaches where it tosses
Its hints of earlier and other creation:
The starfish, the hermit crab, the whale's backbone;
The pools where it offers to our curiosity
The more delicate algæ and the sea anemone.
It tosses up our losses, the torn seine,
The shattered lobsterpot, the broken oar
And the gear of foreign dead men. The sea has many voices,
Many gods and many voices.
                              The salt is on the briar rose,
The fog is in the fir trees.
                         The sea howl
And the sea yelp, are different voices
Often together heard: the whine in the rigging,
The menace and caress of wave that breaks on water,
The distant rota in the granite teeth,
And the wailing warning from the approaching headland
Are all sea voices, and the heaving groaner
Rounded homewards, and the seagull:
And under the oppression of the silent fog
The tolling bell
Measures time not our time, rung by the unhurried
Ground swell, a time
Older than the time of chronometers, older
Than time counted by anxious worried mothers
Lying awake, calculating the future,
Trying to unweave, unwind, unravel
And piece together the past and the future
Between midnight and dawn, when the past is all deception,
The future futureless, before the morning watch
When time stops and time is never ending;
And the ground swell, that is and was from the beginning,
Clangs
The bell.

II

Where is there an end of it, the soundless wailing,
The silent withering of autumn flowers
Dropping their petals and remaining motionless;
Where is there an end to the drifting wreckage,
The prayer of the bone on the beach, the unprayable
Prayer at the calamitous annunciation?

There is no end, but addition: the trailing
Consequence of further days and hours,
While emotion takes to itself the emotionless
Years of living among the breakage
Of what was believed in as the most reliable—
And therefore the fittest for renunciation.

There is the final addition, the failing
Pride or resentment at failing powers,
The unattached devotion which might pass for devotionless,
In a drifting boat with a slow leakage,
The silent listening to the undeniable
Clamour of the bell of the last annunciation.

Where is the end of them, the fishermen sailing
Into the wind's tail, where the fog cowers?
We cannot think of a time that is oceanless
Or of an ocean not littered with wastage
Or of a future that is not liable
Like the past, to have no destination.

We have to think of them as forever bailing,
Setting and hauling, while the North East lowers
Over shallow banks unchanging and erosionless
Or drawing their money, drying sails at dockage;
Not as making a trip that will be unpayable
For a haul that will not bear examination.

There is no end of it, the voiceless wailing,
No end to the withering of withered flowers,
To the movement of pain that is painless and motionless,
To the drift of the sea and the drifting wreckage,
The bone's prayer to Death its God. Only the hardly, barely
    prayable
Prayer of the one Annunciation.

It seems, as one becomes older,
That the past has another pattern, and ceases to be a mere
    sequence—
Or even development: the latter a partial fallacy
Encouraged by superficial notions of evolution,
Which becomes, in the popular mind, a means of disowning
    the past.
The moments of happiness—not the sense of well-being,
Fruition, fulfilment, security or affection,
Or even a very good dinner, but the sudden illumination—
We had the experience, but missed the meaning,
And approach to the meaning restores the experience
In a different form, beyond any meaning
We can assign to happiness. I have said before
That the past experience revived in the meaning
Is not the experience of one life only
But of many generations—not forgetting
Something that is probably quite ineffable:
The backward look behind the assurance
Of recorded history, the backward half-look
Over the shoulder, towards the primitive terror.
Now, we come to discover that the moments of agony
(Whether, or not, due to misunderstanding,
Having hoped for the wrong things or dreaded the wrong
    things,
Is not in question) are likewise permanent
With such permanence as time has. We appreciate this better
In the agony of others, nearly experienced,
Involving ourselves, than in our own.

For our own past is covered by the currents of action,
But the torment of others remains an experience
Unqualified, unworn by subsequent attrition.
People change, and smile: but the agony abides.
Time the destroyer is time the preserver,
Like the river with its cargo of dead negroes, cows and chicken
    coops,
The bitter apple and bite in the apple.
And the ragged rock in the restless waters,
Waves wash over it, fogs conceal it;
On a halcyon day it is merely a monument,
In navigable weather it is always a seamark
To lay a course by: but in the sombre season
Or the sudden fury, is what it always was.

III

I sometimes wonder if that is what Krishna meant—
Among other things—or one way of putting the same thing:
That the future is a faded song, a Royal Rose or a lavender
    spray
Of wistful regret for those who are not yet here to regret,
Pressed between yellow leaves of a book that has never been
    opened.
And the way up is the way down, the way forward is the way
    back.
You cannot face it steadily, but this thing is sure,
That time is no healer: the patient is no longer here.
When the train starts, and the passengers are settled
To fruit, periodicals and business letters
(And those who saw them off have left the platform)
Their faces relax from grief into relief,
To the sleepy rhythm of a hundred hours.
Fare forward, travellers! not escaping from the past
Into different lives, or into any future;
You are not the same people who left that station
Or who will arrive at any terminus,
While the narrowing rails slide together behind you;

And on the deck of the drumming liner
Watching the furrow that widens behind you,
You shall not think ' the past is finished '
Or ' the future is before us '.
At nightfall, in the rigging and the aerial,
Is a voice descanting (though not to the ear,
The murmuring shell of time, and not in any language)
' Fare forward, you who think that you are voyaging;
You are not those who saw the harbour
Receding, or those who will disembark,
Here between the hither and the farther shore
While time is withdrawn, consider the future
And the past with an equal mind.
At the moment which is not of action or inaction
You can receive this: " on whatever sphere of being
The mind of men may be intent
At the time of death "—that is the one action
(And the time of death is every moment)
Which shall fructify in the lives of others:
And do not think of the fruit of action.
Fare forward.
       O voyagers, O seamen,
You who come to port, and you whose bodies
Will suffer the trial and judgment of the sea,
Or whatever event, this is your real destination.'
So Krishna, as when he admonished Arjuna
On the field of battle.
          Not fare well,
But fare forward, voyagers.

IV

Lady, whose shrine stands on the promontory,
Pray for all those who are in ships, those
Whose business has to do with fish, and
Those concerned with every lawful traffic
And those who conduct them.

Repeat a prayer also on behalf of
Women who have seen their sons or husbands
Setting forth and not returning:
Figlia del tuo figlio,
Queen of Heaven.
Also pray for those who were in ships, and
Ended their voyage on the sand, in the sea's lips
Or in the dark throat which will not reject them
Or wherever cannot reach them the sound of the sea bell's
Perpetual angelus.

V

To communicate with Mars, converse with spirits,
To report the behaviour of the sea monster,
Describe the horoscope, haruspicate or scry,
Observe disease in signatures, evoke
Biography from the wrinkles of the palm
And tragedy from fingers; release omens
By sortilege, or tea leaves, riddle the inevitable
With playing cards, fiddle with pentagrams
Or barbituric acids, or dissect
The recurrent image into pre-conscious terrors—
To explore the womb, or tomb, or dreams; all these are usual
Pastimes and drugs, and features of the press:
And always will be, some of them especially
When there is distress of nations and perplexity
Whether on the shores of Asia, or in the Edgeware Road.
Men's curiosity searches past and future
And clings to that dimension. But to apprehend
The point of intersection of the timeless
With time, is an occupation for the saint—
No occupation either, but something given
And taken, in a lifetime's death in love,
Ardour and selflessness and self-surrender.
For most of us, there is only the unattended
Moment, the moment in and out of time,
The distraction fit, lost in a shaft of sunlight,

The wild thyme unseen, or the winter lightning
Or the waterfall, or music heard so deeply
That it is not heard at all, but you are the music
While the music lasts. These are only hints and guesses,
Hints followed by guesses; and the rest
Is prayer, observance, discipline, thought and action.
The hint half-guessed, the gift half-understood, is Incarnation.
Here the impossible union
Of spheres of existence is actual,
Here the past and future
Are conquered, and reconciled,
Where action were otherwise movement
Of that which is only moved
And has in it no source of movement—
Driven by daemonic, chthonic
Powers. And right action is freedom
From past and future also.
For most of us, this is the aim
Never here to be realised;
Who are only undefeated
Because we have gone on trying;
We, content at the last
If our temporal reversion nourish
(Not too far from the yew-tree)
The life of significant soil.

T. S. Eliot

NOTES ON THE POEMS

REALISM AND SATIRE
Poets of the reaction against Georgian Romanticism

RICHARD CHURCH

Reckless: An ironical little poem. The two-stress line, unrhymed, suits the unemotional impersonal comment.

ROBERT GRAVES

Gulls and Men: Robert Graves is a strongly individual poet. Contrast this poem with Herbert Read's *Summer Rain* (p. 23). In the latter it is the sensations that matter; in the former it is the thought. A most unusual and paradoxical thought it is too: lack of foresight, stupidity, is in men, by implication, the quality which often leads to brilliant improvisation; so, since gulls are found to be equally stupid, they therefore must share " this jewel " of creativeness. Where, then, is man's vaunted superiority in the order of created things?

Saint: The allegory of the Red Cross Knight takes us back to Spenser's *Faerie Queene*, but what does he stand for here? Is he man's better nature, while the " Blatant Beast " is his lower nature—a sort of Jekyll and Hyde? Does the conflict stand for the struggle between goodness and sin? Or idealism versus materialism? Do not overlook the significance of the title. Sanctity, remember, is not a gift, but a state to be reached only by the perilous road that leads, beset with temptation, through tracts of desolation and spiritual darkness.

The meaning of the poem is not stated, but only suggested, by the cumulative impressions conveyed by the words. It is a poem to speculate upon. The Beast, for instance, is spoken of humorously and almost affectionately; the Knight, by comparison, seems a poor specimen. Do you now begin to suspect satire? There is no exaltation of man in either of these poems by Graves.

G. ROSTREVOR HAMILTON

The Way Home: Notice the prosaic note struck in the fifth line of the first stanza, by the sudden departure from regular rhythm and rhyme. This is deliberate of course, and emphasizes the lyricism of stanza two, which in turn throws into strong relief the contrasting startling realism of the third stanza.

The Flaking Pineapple: The mixture of prosaic and poetic styles of language is a common feature of modern verse.

EDWIN MUIR

Suburban Dream: See the note in the Foreword (p. 7). This poet's forms are, in the main, traditional, and his style is unimpassioned, clear, and concise.

The Child Dying: This poem has great lyrical beauty. The traditional metre and the rhyme add to it.

HERBERT PALMER

A Fable: This poem is in sharp contrast to *Saint* by Robert Graves. There is allegory here too, but it is humorous and not at all profound. As a fable, it is capable of many applications, either to human beings or to nations. The last stanza has a hint of Russia about it, and a warning against appeasement.

HERBERT READ

Summer Rain: This poet was one of the original Imagist group, and there is evidence of it in his choice of words, his economy of expression, his clear-cut images, and the classical smoothness of his stanzas. Notice that the poem is not, however, written in Free Verse. Neither is it metrical, although many of the lines have a basic four-foot rhythm.

SIEGFRIED SASSOON

The Case for Miners and *At the Cenotaph:* Contrasted with Auden (q.v. below), Sassoon's satire is one degree more restrained; but note the intensity of the fury that is restrained in the last two lines of *The Case for Miners.*

A Flower Has Opened and *Since Thought Is Life:* In contrast again with Auden's pessimism, note the poetic beauty and the optimism of the first of these two poems. Then contrast Sassoon's Christian view of human suffering in the second poem with Auden's desire to eradicate it as an unqualified evil. Sassoon feels pity for " all victims " but glories with " Lorenzo on his grid ", because human suffering reflects and helps to atone for the sufferings of Christ crucified.

ANDREW YOUNG

Field-Glasses and *The Shepherd's Hut:* His language is clear and direct. There is no allusiveness, no symbolism, and no allegory. His is the poetry of an actively observant mind, that picks out detail as clearly as a pair of field-glasses. But, notice in each poem the additional touch of delightful fancy, which raises it above the level of mere recording.

REALISTS OF THE 1930's
Poetry of the Common Man

W. H. AUDEN

The Unknown Citizen: Here the poet satirizes our bureaucratic society, in which the individual is threatened with extinction in a card-index.

The rhythm is interesting, because it is reminiscent of the Sprung Rhythm of Gerard Manly Hopkins. A characteristic common to both is a regular pattern of strongly accented syllables, with an indefinite number of unstressed ones in between. In traditional metrical verse the usual allowance of " slack " syllables is one or two (sometimes three) between stresses. In Sprung Rhythm the lines must be read so that the accents fall at regular intervals. Auden's poem has four stresses in a line, and sometimes as many as four " slacks " between two of them. For example:

And our só-cial Psy- chó-logy wórk-ers fóund
That he was pópular with his mátes and líked a drínk
The préss are con- vínced that he bought a
                                          páper every dáy.

Read the poem with an awareness of this basic four-foot rhythm and you will not want to call it prose.

Musée des Beaux Arts: In Breughel's picture, Icarus is shown sinking below the surface of the sea: nothing can be seen of him but two tiny legs, almost unnoticed in the middle distance. The foreground is taken up by the figure of a man ploughing, and the whole painting shows a world going about its business as usual, oblivious of the tragedy which has just taken place. The theme of the poem, as of the picture, is man's selfish indifference and isolationism.

Notice the power of the calm, unemotional words. This poem is a good example of the effectiveness of under-statement. Icarus, who flew too near the sun so that the heat melted the wax with which his father, Daedalus, had fixed his wings to his shoulders, becomes, in the poem, not a figure in Greek mythology, but a real boy—" a boy falling out of the sky ". So the legend becomes, in a moment, a real and touching incident, and the theme is revealed more vividly in this almost commonplace language, than it would have been in more emotional words.

The poem is written in rhymed, irregular verse, in speech rhythm, not in metre. If you think it might just as well have been written as a prose passage, notice how much emphasis would have been lost. Examine each line and see why the poet broke off where he did; notice that at the end of a line we find either a strong emphasis weighted by a rhyme (as " waiting " and " skating "), or the thought is held up for a moment before making an impact all the stronger at the beginning of the next line (as with " Children ", " Scratches " and " Water "). Look at the line: " They never forgot "; by making that into one complete line, the poet gets a double meaning, for, before we link it up with its grammatical object in the next line (" That even the dreadful martyrdom must run its course "), the statement registers complete finality in one terse sentence.

O What Is That Sound? Modern man caught up in the war machine is poignantly indicated in this ballad. Very successful it is too as a ballad, having many of the characteristics of the genuine old folk-poem: economical narrative, repetition of word and pattern, alternate question and answer, and the fear coming nearer step by step until it is upon us in a climax of horror.

Refugee Blues: This well illustrates Auden's fellow-feeling for the oppressed of whatever race or creed. The emotion is made almost unbearably poignant by the lifeless monotony that we hear in the voice of the old man.

JOHN BETJEMAN

In Westminster Abbey: A good example of the light, ironical verse written by this poet.

ROY CAMPBELL

The Birth of Christ: This poem is translated from a Spanish poem of the great Christian mystic of the late sixteenth century, St. John of the Cross. It is one of a series of

"Romances" based upon St. John's Gospel: "In the beginning was the Word, and the Word was with God, and the Word was God . . . And the Word was made Flesh, and dwelt among us. . . ." The poem quoted here is "*Romance IX*", and it concludes the series.

"His beloved" (line 5) and "the bride" (line 22) are symbolical references to Christ's human nature.

"the wondrous marriage" (line 13) refers to the union of the two natures, human and divine, in Christ after the Incarnation.

The last stanza refers to the sublime paradox of Christian truth, that God should become Man.

Washing Day: Roy Campbell is capable of savage satire, but here there is nothing but fancy. Notice the inevitability of every word and phrase. He mixes colloquialisms and literary language in a perfect harmony. Look at the verbal felicity of "dizzy choreography" and:

"Inflate themselves and dance upon the line";
and
"As if there were religion in a string".

Listen to the rhythm of: "They curtsey and collapse, revolve and billow". And notice the animation given to the poem by the alternate double rhymes.

C. DAY LEWIS

The Stand-To, Will It Be So Again? and *Word Over All:* All three poems by Cecil Day Lewis are connected with the 1939 war. "*Stand-To*" commemorates the invasion threat in the autumn of 1940, when reports circulated that invasion barges had actually left the coast of France and were approaching the south coast of England. Whether the reports were true or not, certainly one September night the alarm was given, the invasion plan was put into force, and all troops and Home Guard units in the southern counties stood at their action stations the whole night through.

The other two poems have great beauty of rhythm and language. *Word Over All* is particularly musical and satisfying to articulate. C. Day Lewis has, like many others, returned in his later poems to more traditional forms, to regular rhythm and to rhyme. No attempt, however, should be made to " scan " these lines and divide them into feet. When they are read with an appreciation of their speech-rhythm, the words fall into a pattern of alternate stress and no-stress, of themselves.

In *Word Over All* see if you can appreciate the division into lines. Can you see, for example, how much more musical and effective are lines 7 and 8, divided as they are, than if a conventional metrical division had been made at " surge ", as:

How shall the sea-waif, who lives from surge to surge,
Chart current and reef aright?

Without the Free Verse movement to loosen up the structure of verse, *that* is how those two lines might have been written.

LOUIS MACNEICE

Louis MacNeice is as brilliantly witty, as colloquially attractive as Auden, but he seems to have less of the passionate feeling which underlies Auden's ironical flippancy.

Prayer Before Birth is a good example of his almost slick skill with words and rhythm. Precisely because of this facility, his verses are fun, and delightful to the ear: so much so, that the satire does not register. All the better. If we have to choose between satire and fun, let us have the fun. Notice that we do not say that about Auden's poems, because we sense in them a deep seriousness which we have to respect. That is the difference between Auden and MacNeice.

Flight of the Heart is a ballad written in anything but a realistic style. Clues to the theme lie in the phrase: "lame dogs" and in the tower—not an ivory one, but something much more material.

Spring Voices is an example of the contempt these poets had for the harmless bourgeois citizen—"the small householder". The danger of poetry is that it is so persuasive. We read a poem like this and laugh with the poet, only to find that often we are mocking ourselves. Anyway, this poem is out of date, for since 1939 none of us is safe and cautious with a comfortable bank-balance and a neat, closed home: we are all gamblers with life, willy-nilly.

WILLIAM PLOMER

September Evening, 1938: The threat of war came very close in September 1938, and sharpened one's appreciation of the simple things of everyday life which suddenly became infinitely precious under the threat to their permanency. There is something very touching in the utter simplicity of language and thought in this poem, and in the sudden intimate, homely touch of George and his girl.

STEPHEN SPENDER

To Poets and Airmen and *The Air Raid across the Bay:* In Stephen Spender, satire has softened into pity, which has in it a touch of hopelessness. The two poems quoted here were written early in the war when air raids and airmen were in the forefront of our minds. There is no easy colloquialism here; on the other hand, there is no "poetic diction" either. The language of everyday speech is used, but notice how the writer transmutes into poetry the prosaic terms of geometry.

NEW ROMANTIC MOVEMENT
Embracing Symbolism and Surrealism

GEORGE BARKER

Calamiterror: This is Part X of the long poem which
is a vividly impressionistic portrayal of the world in
1936 as the poet saw it. In July of that year the Spanish
Civil War began between the forces of the " Right "
helped by Nazi Germany and Fascist Italy, and the
Popular Front Government forces, helped by Communists. In the struggle between two extremes of political
and religious beliefs (so extreme that Britain could support
neither) the government army was defeated, and General
Franco was made Dictator. Terrible as this conflict
seemed at the time, it was to prove only a curtain-raiser
to the more fearful drama of the Second World War;
but while it lasted, it fired with idealistic zeal (for both
parties) many young Englishmen, and particularly poets,
many of whom became active participants in the war.
The varying phases and battles and destroyed towns
(Guernica, Barcelona, Irun) became symbols of the
struggle for the liberation of the people on the one hand,
or of the fight against Communism on the other.

It is easy to see which side George Barker is on. He
sees the common man all over the world shedding his
blood in the cause of freedom from tyranny and exploita-
tion. The miners and workmen in Spain, England,
America, and Wales are the victims of the Calamity and
the Terror of the title.

The poem is full of symbolism and vivid imagery:

" I see England
With the underground mines run bleeding along
     her like wounds."

Notice the surrealistic image in which the petals of a
rose are seen as tongues. Notice also the recurring image

of blood in the red rose, the crimson heart of the fuschia, the poppy (emblem of the 1914-18 war), and the swan pecking her breast like the pelican, for blood to feed her young.

The poet takes into himself the suffering of his fellow-men: he is all of them:

" And my mother world, with bomb-holes in her
        bosom,
Goes gradually on, with the myriad of me at her
        breast."

As well as the vivid imagery, note the lovely sound in lines like:

" But the whipporwill wends his way through the
        Wyoming woods ".

PAUL DEHN

Lament for a Sailor: Here the effect is obtained by sugges-tive words whose effect is cumulative: sea-water, spars, swimming, mackerel tide, dolphins, shoal—all these unite to create both an image of the starry, moonlit sky and the sea above the drowned sailor. The double image is continued in the second stanza where moths in the air are like " flies " on the fisherman's line, and where the clouds moving across the sky are the shapes of silent ships moving above the depths of the ocean.

The delight of the poem, apart from the dreamlike quality of this imagery, is in the smooth rhythm, the rhymes, and above all the peculiar charm of the words in the last stanza: " my ghost, my grayling " (the last a word which is not merely the name of a fish, but ob-viously a term of endearment); and the wonderfully expressive " fat-knuckled, noisy diver ".

This poem is a good example of the use of suggestive words: the whole picture of the drowned sailor is con-veyed simply through a succession of sea and sky images.

Habitué: This is a poignant and almost cruel piece of observation. It is a repulsive picture of an old roué, with his " ebbing hair " and " pink and pug-dog eye ", forced to recognize that his day is done; yet at the same time it is full of pathos.

Notice the originality of the phrase " crow's-feet ago ", and see how much is conveyed by the pun on " grave " in the last line but one.

Lawrence Durrell

On Ithaca Standing: Ulysses' home was the little rocky island of Ithaca, to which he returned at last after the long siege of Troy and his ten years' wandering on the sea. Notice the suggestiveness of the metaphors of crucifixion in which the body is the nail, the heart the anvil on which it is beaten out, and the island the cross.

The rhythm is speech rhythm and there are occasional half rhymes: " glass . . . was ", " diamonds . . . hands ". The only true rhyme is not a very happy one: " crucifix . . . licks ".

Clifford Dyment

Pieta: The title of this poem is that given to the Mother of God bearing in her arms the dead body of Christ after it has been taken down from the Cross. The similes in lines 3 and 5 are homely but original and vivid.

Roy Fuller

The Divided Life Re-Lived: At a first reading this seems to have a very prosaic rhythm, but one soon becomes aware of the basic four and three stresses in alternate lines. It is interesting to note that there is a regular pattern of syllables, every odd line having fifteen and every even line eleven.

The theme of the poem is the return, after war, to a mood of disillusion at everything being just the same as before—it is the same old world of " cod ", that is, of humbugging ourselves and other people.

DAVID GASCOYNE

A Tough Generation: This is interesting as showing the contrast between the later and the earlier work of a surrealist poet (see the poem translated by Gascoyne on p. 10 of the Foreword). In his maturity he has abandoned extravagance, exaggeration, and obscurity, and here writes a perfectly straightforward poem in blank verse. This illustrates the tendency of even the most revolutionary poets to return to traditional forms.

The theme: the uncertain state of the world has re-established the primitive law of " every man for himself ". The present " tough generation " has grown up in " a wood of rotted trees " any of which may fall and destroy life. This is no time for idealism: self-interest is man's chief concern. So the poet sadly comments on life to-day, and thankfully contemplates the few remaining manifestations of beauty.

SEÁN JENNETT

Café au Lait: In most modern poems the reader has to be on the alert, ready to keep up with the poet's thought as it changes direction and mood at lightning speed. The startling realization and the contrast in stanza two of this poem, illustrate very well the poet's economy in expressing his thought without laborious linking-up and filling-in. This economy is not so new as it seems, for it is a feature of old ballads.

Christ's Cross Grows Wings: This is a poem to test your receptiveness. Allow the images to crowd into your mind; pick out the words which suggest war and bombing. " Christ's cross grows wings "—do you see an aeroplane, or a Nazi swastika (a later clue is given in the reference to Christ's " usurped symbol ")? " Christ's man " is mankind.

FRANCIS KING

The Martyr: Do not attempt to wrest a " meaning " from this in the sense of a paraphrase. The thought in your mind should be: " I am the martyr; these are *my* hands, *my* head, *my* heart, *my* body." Thus the reader identifies himself with the poet and shares the emotion which inspired the poem.

JAMES KIRKUP

The Drowned Sailor: This extract, brief though it is, shows the poet's economy and vividness in word and image.

LAURIE LEE

Bird and *Christmas Landscape:* These poems are full of brilliant flashes of imagery and exciting words. The thought is suggested through symbols and sparkling images. There are some wonderfully eloquent phrases: " her singing cage of bone ", " the webbed wings of her hand ", " the ground bitter with stones ", and, vividly lighting up the Christmas tree: " the fir tree warms to a bloom of candles ".

W. R. RODGERS

Autumn Day: This poem gives ample evidence of the influence of Gerard Manly Hopkins on the language of poetry. The exuberant inventiveness, the rich alliteration and assonance, and the copious rhymes are as fresh as they were in Hopkins's poetry a hundred years ago. This is no mere imitation, however, and Rodgers has plenty to add in his own twentieth-century manner, especially in his playing with words and making them work overtime with unexpected supplementary meanings

Notice, for example, the secondary reading of: " sticking bones shockingly unkinned", where the alliteration forces our ears to supply an " s " in the last word; and " whirl-spools of light", where the unexpected " s " forces the eye to look upward away from water level to which the previous image had directed it. Notice, too, the pun on " reports " which are " garbled " and then are associated with guns.

The vivid images in the last two lines illustrate the skill of Rodgers, who, like other poets of his period (and this is conspicuously true of Dylan Thomas) not only makes words give up every scintilla of meaning, but loads them with implications and images so that they expand in the imagination.

DYLAN THOMAS

He is one of the most difficult of this group of Romantic poets, although it is to be noted that his later verse is more lucid than his earlier work owing to his greater control over language. His poetry consists of a succession of images, but they are not unorganized as they would be in a surrealist poem. He says himself that a poem starts with an image which arises from his emotions. This image is not allowed expression at white heat, but is carefully and critically examined until the poet finds in what direction it can be developed. The first image calls up another which may appear quite irrelevant, and then between the two apparently unrelated images, a subconscious relationship emerges, and a third image is born. His poems are thus based on images whose relevance and connection the reader may find it difficult to discern. The important thing to remember, however, is that this is not merely random recording of the images that rise up in the mind, but that it is a highly complex method by which the poet strives to write down the complexity of his thoughts. Edith Sitwell, commenting on his second book of poems in 1926, wrote of the " poignant and moving beauty " of his images; and

11

Herbert Read, reviewing another collection of poems in 1939, said that they contained "the most absolute poetry" written in our time. The poet himself, in a note prefacing his *Collected Poems, 1934-1952*, writes: "These poems, with all their crudities, doubts, and confusions, are written for the love of Man and in praise of God. . . ."

Dawn Raid: The initial image is born from an emotion of pity, but from that, through a series of images rising from "the burst pavement of stone" where the old man lies dead, to the sky where "the morning is flying on the wings of his age", the poem changes to a triumphal song, in which the bomb that killed him, honours him. He had lived for a hundred years, so no ordinary death for him, with the slow decay of the grave. A cataclysm was sent from heaven to give him rebirth into eternity.

To Others Than You: Notice the strong surrealistic flavour of the images (for example, a false coin staring from an eye-socket), but notice too how they are organized and unified to convey a picture of deceit and falsehood. They are images of conjuring, illusion, and counterfeiting: "bad coin", "palmed the lie", "worked by mirrors", "quickness of hand". The unfamiliar and startling relation given to unlike objects is definitely surrealist in effect.

With a poem like this, it is enough to take the poet's words and allow yourself to be subject to the sensations they give rise to. Feel for yourself the horrid jar as your teeth bite on the unexpected hard fragment in the soft sweet; blush in your own sensitiveness at the mockery which is no respecter of your reticence. It is impossible to give expression to all the sensations one gets from this poem, and it is foolish to try. There is no bigger obstacle to appreciating a poem, than to feel compelled to paraphrase what the poet has written. Even if the thought of a poem is of paramount importance, all that is necessary is comprehension of the meaning: a translation is not called for. On the other hand, if the sensations and emotions are predominant, all the more reason for being content to experience them.

Fern Hill: It would be hard to find a better example of " absolute poetry " than this. It is the concentrated essence of all the bounding happiness of every child who ever spent a summer holiday on a farm. The affinity with Gerard Manly Hopkins is evident, but the idiom of his imagery is Thomas's individual contribution to the poetry of to-day. In his hands clichés are given a new face: " happy as the grass was green ", " happy as the heart was long ", " once below a time ", " all the sun long ", " all the moon long ". There is something of Edith Sitwell, too, in his use and transference of epithets.

TERENCE TILLER

The Fool in " Lear ": The fool in *King Lear* is the bitter, jibing commentator on the king's folly in banishing one daughter and giving away all his kingdom to the other two; he is the " sad wasp ". Then he is a frightened child crying for cold and loneliness; and then he disappears from the play. The fool may be interpreted as an embodiment of the king's misgivings and fears, all of which ceased when he lost his wits, and so the fool vanished too. The poem suggests this thought in lovely strange images that bring to life the poor, sad, mocking, terrified boy.

Only once, towards the end of the play, is the fool mentioned again, and that is when Lear, holding in his arms the dead body of Cordelia, for a moment mistakes her for the fool, and says: " And my poor fool is hang'd!" For this moment the fool exists again in Terence Tiller's poem:

> . . . it was in me he wrapped
> Cordelia, one hour before I slipped
>   into the cold again.

Beggar: Notice how the poet builds up these pictures in words. Never forget that words are the poet's material, and that a pondering over his words often provides the clue to an obscure poem. Here in this simple and touching portrait of the beggar, you should linger over images like: " old as a coat on a chair ", " his eyes white pebbles blind with deserts ", " feathers of rags and rags of body ".

Camels: In the same way as in *Beggar*, pick out the most eloquent phrases.

HENRY TREECE

A Thief to His Lord: Here is surrealist influence, but the poem is not at all complex. Here is a simple idea, expressed in simple sonnet form, in racy and colloquial language.

Lyric: This is a little poem full of tenderness and the beauty of flowers. Be aware of the delicate alliteration.

LAURENCE WHISTLER

Flight: The title of this poem states the theme quite clearly. Notice the suggestion of attacking aircraft in the first three lines. There are some eloquent phrases: " A flicker of bony fingers here and there ", " A big moth saying nothing in grey air ", " the mere innuendo of wings ", " the cry of the lost in the luminous valley ".

RETURN TO NATURALISM
Poets of comment upon the Contemporary Scene

LILIAN BOWES LYON

Stone Pity: This poem of love and pity has a beautiful, long-phrased rhythm.

Northumbrian Farm: Pick out lovely vivid images like: " hands unwind The silk-soft milk, the frothing fairy skein "; and note the anger against sporting " Gentlemen of England now abed " and the pity for the " half-shot-away hare " whose blood, staining the grass,

> Stitches a precious thread
> Of blood into the upland turf.

These two poems, as well as many others in this section, answer those who would deny that there is any beauty in the poetry of to-day.

NORMAN NICHOLSON

Cleator Moor, Bombing Practice, The Tame Hare, and *The Undiscovered Planet:* Here is a fine young poet who writes of the Cumberland dales and lakes as one who is, in bone and blood, native to the place. There is no narrow outlook here, but a penetrating and sympathetic insight into the very heart of the people who are one with the place. The poet is intimate with both; his observation and his vivid imagination illuminate the scene with witty and original epithets.

HENRY REED

Movement of Bodies: This poem will be appreciated most by those who have done their military service. They will recognize the sergeant instructing the raw " intake " in tactics. It is an amusing parody of the sergeant-instructor's diction; but the poet's mood is serious. What the instructor sees as " bodies " to be moved about as counters by " those up above ", the poet sees as poor young raw recruits, untutored in war and unused to the callous impersonality of it.

ALAN ROSS

Guidebooks: This is an example of the prosaic style used by many contemporary poets. The unemotional language seems to give a smouldering intensity to the strong emotion lying beneath the commonplace words.

STANLEY SNAITH

Hiroshima: On 6th August, 1945, was dropped the first atom bomb, on Hiroshima in Japan. It brought to a dreadful end the Second World War and inaugurated a new era of horror and fear, in which man faces the possibility of total extinction.

HAL SUMMERS

Homage to Thor Heyerdahl: The hero of the poem is a young Norwegian who set out, with five other adventurous Scandinavians, to prove that the Polynesian islands had been colonized from Peru. His theory was dismissed by all authorities as being impossible, since no primitive craft was capable of transporting large numbers of people from Peru across the trackless Pacific. To establish the truth of his belief, he and his companions set sail on a light balsa-wood raft, copied exactly from descriptions of the rafts used by the early Peruvians. After three months they reached one of the Polynesian groups of islands, and after wrecking their raft on the coral reef, succeeded in reaching the shore. The Kon-Tiki expedition, named after Tiki the Sun-God, a representation of whose face decorated the mainsail, is an epic adventure, which shows that half-way through the twentieth century, the Viking spirit is not dead.

Prologue to a Theatrical Season: In life there is no certainty, but on the stage everything goes according to plan: the ends of actions are determined beforehand. In real life it is hard to see how things are connected, but life on the stage is a carefully selected sequence of events, logically arranged. The play has no reality save what the auditor gives it, but he, on the other hand, absorbed in the play, lives in it another complete life.

RUTHVEN TODD

These Are Facts: During the war there was much controversy on the subject of to bomb or not to bomb cities which contained architectural treasures of the past. Those who deplored the ruin of many of London's lovely churches were attacked, as this poet attacks them, on the grounds that " people are more than places ". This is the obvious view to take amid the stresses of war. Nevertheless, men's bodies are mortal and yet may reproduce their kind, whereas a work of art is unique: it is intended to last as long as the material substances of which it is made, and, once destroyed, it cannot be reproduced.

It Was Easier: Notice again, in this as in so many poems in this section, the use of commonplace, everyday language which, instead of lessening the impact of the poet's thought, thrusts it upon us with grim emphasis (as in the vivid and startling image in the last line).

Dorothy Wellesley

Docks and *The Traffic Problem in East Anglia:* The poet writes with interest, close observation, and love of the contemporary scene.

Back to the House: There is lovely rhythm and sound in this poem.

REBIRTH OF SIMPLE LYRICISM
Poems of Love, Hope, and Faith

Frances Bellerby

The Summer Dove: The delayed action of grief is experienced here with authentic and poignant suddenness in the last four lines.

Genesis: This is a deeply spiritual poem—a cry for understanding of life which begins in love and ends in death.

Edmund Blunden

Two Small Elegies: These are typical of the close and tender observation of nature, and the lyrical quality of this poet.

After the Bombing: Many poets have been inspired by the theme outlined in the first two stanzas: the destruction of nature by man and nature's ultimate triumph. But none dreamed that man with his genius for destruction would reinstate exuberant nature in the heart of a city, as was so often seen in the riot of flowers which sprang up with such alacrity on bombed sites.

WALTER DE LA MARE

Listen, But Oh My Dear, And So to Bed, and *An Island:* Walter de la Mare is one of the greatest poets of this century. He is the poet of magic, of music, of verbal enchantment, and of beauty.

KENNETH GEE

Time and the Ocean: The experience related here is unusual, in that it reverses the conventional home-coming of the exile. Strung up to meet sadness and change, he finds an indifference in the very lack of change that chills him to the heart.

JOHN MASEFIELD

Delight in Water and *February Night:* Masefield's tranquil verse with its limpid beauty is the expression of a serene, gentle wisdom.

AVERIL MORLEY

Lapwings in March: The very word " lapwing " has an exultant beauty which rouses an emotion in the reader even before the poet has given expression to hers.

The Baby: What better subject could there be for a young mother to write about than the miracle of new life that she sees in her baby? In this poem the emphasis is not, however, on the tragedy of losing a baby so soon after birth (though that is eloquently implicit in the first stanza) but on the immensity and wonder of God's universe and man's world which the baby inherited and lost so soon.

Ruth Pitter

Fair is the Water and *Thanksgiving for a Fair Summer:* Both these poems show the poet's love of the countryside. In the first she sings her " quiet stave " in thanksgiving for what is indeed a rarity—" a fair summer ". In the second, notice the attractive rhythm and pattern.

John Pudney

So I Praise These: This is a poem in praise of the heroic " few "—the fighter-pilots of the Battle of Britain—and the country which bore and bred them.

Kathleen Raine

Prayer, The Rose, and *Ecce Homo:* Kathleen Raine is a very considerable poet, whose verse is evocative, deeply sincere, and lyrically perfect. Her poems have great beauty of word and rhythm.

Anne Ridler

For This Time: This is a simple and impressive act of faith and hope, beginning with an echo of one well-known hymn, and ending with a touching little parody of a child's night prayer: " Teach me to live that I may dread the grave as little as my bed ".

A. L. Rowse

Cornish Landscape: This short poem contains the whole essence of a lyric—that leaping-up of the heart of which Wordsworth wrote in:

> My heart leaps up when I behold
> A rainbow in the sky.

E. J. Scovell

A Blue Day: Pick out all the words which give you the colours of shore and sky.

The Giraffe: This poem is full of startling images of which " tulip-stalk " is the first. Notice how the giraffe's height is emphasized.

Rex Warner

Longtailed Tit: Read this without pausing except at the ends of lines. The poem is full of swift, darting words as the spinney is full of birds.

Poem: Contrast the speed of this poem with that of the previous one. This is contemplative where the other is full of movement.

Vernon Watkins

Ophelia and *Wind and Rain:* His poems have a rich, exuberant, Celtic music. This is evident in the first of these two poems, with the insistent, passionate rhythm of the long lines.

Margaret Willy

Good Friday in War: Poetry is the most powerful and the most compact form of speech. This is a good example of a poet's power to pack a wealth of experience and emotion into eight short lines. Notice the beauty of the four " d " sounds in the last line.

ROMANTIC AND INTELLECTUAL
Two great poets

Edith Sitwell

Still Falls the Rain: A rain of bombs fell on London in 1940, but this rain is more than literally a shower of bombs. Behind the monotone of the falling rain is the figure of the crucified Christ, crucified again, in 1940, by the sins of man. In the falling rain we hear the heart-beats of the Man on the Cross, and then the regular beat becomes the hammer blows as the nails are driven home. The Rain is now the rain of sin upon the world —the same sin that betrayed Christ to his murderers—the sin of Cain and of Judas and of every man who turns his hand against his fellow-man. Each day Sin crucifies the Son of God; all of us, rich and poor, are guilty and must cry for mercy.

Now the Rain is the blood of Christ, drained from a heart bursting with pity for the sufferings of all creatures. His Blood is now the ransom paid to expiate man's guilt.

Then comes the desperate cry of Faustus, who knew that even at the eleventh hour Christ's blood could save him from Lucifer: "O Ile leape up to my God". The poem ends with a renewal of Christ's love and mercy.

Dirge for the New Sunrise: This poem is a cry of desolation and anguish at the supreme folly of modern man in letting loose the terrors consequent upon the first atomic bomb. Edith Sitwell feels with all the compassion of which a poet is capable; the war affected her profoundly, shaking her out of the aloofness and exclusiveness which coloured her poetry, gay and delightful as it was. The war brought her to her full stature as a poet.

The Shadow of Cain: The poem from which these two short extracts are taken must be read in full. Here it is impossible to do more than give a hint of its dramatic power and poetic magnificence. In it the poet castigates men for the sin of Cain against Abel, for the hate and envy, the lust for power and gold, which set brother against brother.

There is a great deal of symbolism (a mixture of surrealist and Christian symbolism): the "Whiteness" of the Bread, the Dead and the Claw, is the whiteness of leprosy, corruption, and death. The thunders are "emerald" as are the rainbows in the City of Cain, the green symbolizing both envy and youth.

Then comes a vivid impression of the explosion of the first atomic bomb: "the Primal Matter" was broken; man signed his own death-warrant; and from the explosion "a totem pole of dust arose in memory of Man".

In the later extract, after Lazarus has been used as a

symbol of the spiritual regeneration of man, and Dives
as representing lust for wealth and power, the latter is
accused of the crime of Adam, of Cain, of Sodom, and
of Judas. The poem ends with a passionate denunciation
of man for the evil he has wrought. It has called down
upon him the vengeance of God, "the terrible Rain".
And yet, Christ's mercy is still ready to be poured out
for man in his need:

> And yet—who dreamed that Christ has died in vain?
> He walks again on the Seas of Blood, He comes in
>   the terrible Rain.

T. S. ELIOT

Edith Sitwell's post-war poetry is deeply emotional,
and it is poured out in a resounding and reverberating
free rhythm. Eliot's poetry is the reverse: it arises from
the focusing of a powerful mind upon a deeply troubled
spirit, and emerges impersonal and analytical in mood.
It is equally restrained in form. He has abandoned Free
Verse, and shows a preference for a strong four-stress
line, with a cadence peculiarly his own.

His poetry is profound and needs to be studied. That
is not to say, however, that it has no lyrical quality and
cannot be enjoyed at a first hearing. But it certainly cannot
be understood through the ear alone. It is difficult,
though not invariably so; and the student who is not
hampered by the necessity of attempting the impossible
(the translation of Eliot into the words of a lesser man),
can, by intuition, and with a little help, catch something
of the thought and mood of the poet. For those who
desire to study Eliot's work more deeply, many books
on the subject are available.

The Rock: A play in verse. *The Rock* is the Church (from
the words of Christ: "Thou are Peter, and upon this
Rock I will build my Church"). The passage quoted
satirizes our present-day pagan and materialistic outlook,
and plainly states the need for a return to spirituality.

A Song for Simeon: Running through the poem are the words of old Simeon, who, having prayed that he might live to behold the Messiah, experiences the supreme pleasure of holding the Infant in his arms, and then in this lovely canticle prays to be allowed to die:

> " Lord, now lettest thou thy servant depart in peace, according to thy word:
> For mine eyes have seen thy salvation,
> Which thou hast prepared before the face of all people;
> A light to lighten the Gentiles, and the glory of thy people Israel."

The Dry Salvages: This is one of the *Four Quartets*. These are four profoundly philosophical poems, full of seeking and questioning, but moving with deep certainty and conviction towards the statement of the poet's belief in Christ as God, and in Christianity as the rock on which man's life must be founded, if it is to be a life and not merely a drifting from non-being through existence to extinction.

All four poems take their names from places. The title *The Dry Salvages* is the name of a group of rocks off the coast of Massachusetts.

For the task the poet has set himself, he needs words; and in each of the four poems reference is made to the difficulty of making words work for the poet—they are elusive, they are unreliable and change their meaning; they are tardy and the thought is always ahead of the words needed to express it. Or they are unworthy, constantly degenerating and falling short of the great work required of them—a work which is not merely the precise definition of passionate feeling, but the unifying and disciplining of incoherent emotions and their presentation with illuminating clarity. Words, for Eliot, are not the material in which he shapes and embellishes his thought; they are the very skeleton of which his thoughts are the flesh.

To illustrate Eliot's preoccupation with words, let us

look closely at the sestina* at the beginning of the second movement.

Notice the patterns of the rhymes, which link together and unify all six stanzas: each line in the first stanza rhymes with the corresponding line in every other stanza. Taking them in order, notice the cumulative effect of each group of rhymes:

(a) *Wailing, trailing, failing, sailing, bailing,* and, completing the circle, *wailing* once again. They add up to an impression of despair, ineffectuality, futility.

Notice also other key words: *withering, dropping, remaining, drifting*—complete passivity, no action, no decision.

(b) The second lines all end in the syllable "-less"; all is negative; there is nothing positive: *motionless, emotionless, devotionless, oceanless, erosionless,* and, again completing the circle, *motionless.*

(c) The rhymes in the third lines disintegrate into the finality of the scrapheap: *wreckage, breakage, leakage, wastage, dockage, wreckage.*

(d) Now comes definiteness: *unprayable* at first, but then: *reliable, undeniable, liable,* lapsing into *unpayable* and ending with *barely prayable.* These add up to a sense of duty, of obligation, of insistence on belief and prayer, leading to the sacrifice of self which is implicit in the final group of rhymes:

(e) *annunciation, renunciation, destination, examination,* and ending with the promise of the Incarnation, in the "*one Annunciation*".

There are many other keywords, which build up to a climax, and then fall away towards the close. First, words connected with sound: *soundless wailing, silent withering, silent listening,* and then the climax of *clamour*

---

* It is to be noted that this is a variation of the sestina which normally consist "of six six-line stanzas (with an envoy) in which the line-endings of the first stanza are repeated, but in different order, in the other five".—O.E.D.

of the bell, falling away to *voiceless wailing*. Then there are words connected with movement: *motionless, drifting, trailing, sailing, bailing, setting,* and *hauling* (these last four suggesting the first definite action, but it only leads to: *drawing their money* and *drying sails at dockage*) and then we are back at *the drift of the sea and the drifting wreckage*.

It is aimless movement backwards and forwards, with no goal or purpose. There is no hope in the weary question or answer with which each stanza opens:

> Where is there an end of it?
> There is no end, but addition. . . .
> There is the final addition. . . .
> Where is the end of them . . . ?
> We have to think of them as forever bailing. . . .
> There is no end of it. . . .

Here again is Eliot's preoccupation with Time and Eternity. He has said it all before and will say it again.

The student will find all the help he needs for further study of this poem in: *Four Quartets Rehearsed* (1946) by Raymond Preston, and in *Four Quartets: A Commentary* by Helen L. Gardner (included in *T. S. Eliot—a Study of his Writing by Several Hands* (1947), edited by B. Rajan.

NOTES ON THE POETS

AUDEN, WYSTAN HUGH

Born on Feb. 21, 1907, in York, the son of a doctor, and educated at Gresham's School, Holt, and Christ Church College, Oxford. At university his political sympathies were with the Left and he was associated with a group of young poets, many of whom were Communists. He drove an ambulance in the Spanish Civil War for the Revolutionary armed forces. He married the daughter of Thomas Mann, great German novelist. In 1937 he was awarded the King's Poetry Medal. In 1939 he went to U.S.A. and has since become a naturalized American citizen. Recent publications: *Selected Poems* (1940); *Another Time* (1940); *New Year Letter* (1941); *For the Time Being* (1945); *Collected Shorter Poems, 1930-1944* (1950); *Nones* (1952).

BARKER, GEORGE

Born in Feb. 1913 and educated at Marlborough Road L.C.C. School and Regent St. Polytechnic. He published his first book in 1933, and was Professor of Literature in Tokyo University in 1939. He lived in America until 1943, but returned to England where he lives in the country. Recent publications: *Calamiterror* (1937)—directly inspired by the Spanish Civil War; *Lament and Triumph* (1940); *Eros in Dogma* (1944); *News of the World* (1950); *The Dead Seagull* (1950); *The True Confession of George Barker* (1950).

BELLERBY, FRANCES

Born in the West country but partly of Welsh extraction. She now lives in Devonshire on the edge of Dartmoor, after thirteen years in Cornwall on the edge of Bodmin Moor. Her lifelong outstanding interests are poetry and animals; her chief occupation is the writing of poetry and of occasional short stories. Her publications include two books of verse, *Plash Mill* (1947) and *The Brightening Cloud* (1950); one novel, *Hath the Rain a Father?* (1947); three books of short stories, *Come to an End* (1939), *The Acorn and the Cup* (1948), and *A Breathless Child* (1952).

BETJEMAN, JOHN

Born in 1906 and educated at Marlborough and Oxford, where he was a contemporary of Auden and MacNeice. He is an extremely versatile writer. He was U.K. Press Attaché in Dublin, 1941–3; was attached to the Admiralty, 1944; and is now book critic for the *Daily Herald*. His publications (with John Piper) include the *Buckinghamshire Guide* (1948) and *Berkshire Guide* (1949), and the *Shell Guide to Shropshire* (1951). His books of verse include *Old Lights for New Chancels* (1940); *New Bats in Old Belfries* (1945); and *Selected Poems* (1948). His interest in architecture is well illustrated by his book *Ghastly Good Taste*, 1933. A collection of his essays under the title *First and Last Loves* was published in 1952.

BLUNDEN, EDMUND CHARLES

Born in 1896 at Yalding, near Maidstone, and educated at Cleave's Grammar School, Yalding, Christ's Hospital, and Queen's College, Oxford. He served overseas in the First World War with the Royal Sussex Regt., was gassed, and received the M.C. He was Professor of Literature in Tokyo University, and cultural adviser to the British Embassy between 1924 and 1927. Since 1931 he has been a Fellow and Tutor of Merton College, Oxford. In 1948 he was in Japan as a member of the United Kingdom Liaison Mission. His first poems were published in 1914. His later publications include two books of verse, *Shells by a Stream* (1944), and *After the Bombing* (1949); and the prose works, *English Villages* (1941), *Thomas Hardy* (1942), *Cricket Country* (1944), and *Shelley, A Life Story* (1946).

CAMPBELL, ROY

Born in 1901 in Durban, the son of Dr. Samuel George Campbell. At the age of 15 he joined up in the South African Infantry in the First World War but was sent back to school. After his education in South Africa he went to Oxford. Between the wars he lived for some time in Wales and some time in France, always living the rough, active life of the country people. In the Camargue he became a professional bull-fighter, steer-thrower and horse-dealer. He served in Franco's army in the Spanish Civil War, and was war correspondent of the London Catholic newspaper, *The Tablet*. In the Second World War he was permanently disabled. His published books of verse include *The Flaming Terrapin* (1924); *Adamastor* (1928); *The Georgiad* (1931); *Flowering Reeds* (1933); *Mithraic Emblems* (1936); *Talking Bronco* (1946); *Collected Poems* (1949); *Saint John of the Cross* (1951), translated from the Spanish; *Baudelaire: Les Fleurs du Mal* (1952), translated from the French. His autobiography, *Light on a Dark Horse*, was published in 1951.

CHURCH, RICHARD

Born in 1893 in London and educated at Dulwich Hamlet School. He was a Civil Servant for twenty-four years but became literary adviser and reader to Dent's, the publishing firm, and has been examiner in Voice-Production and Verse-Speaking at the University of London. He is both poet and novelist; his novel *The Porch* (1937) was awarded the Femina Vie Heureuse Prize for 1938. He has published numerous novels and more than twelve books of verse, including *Collected Poems* (1948) and *Selected Lyrical Poems* (1951).

DEHN, PAUL

Born in 1912 and educated at Shrewsbury and Brasenose College, Oxford. He is film-critic to the *Sunday Chronicle*, and has collaborated in scenarios for films. His published volumes of poetry include *The Day's Alarm* (1949) and *Romantic Landscape* (1952).

DE LA MARE, WALTER

Born in 1873 in the Kentish village of Charlton and educated at St. Paul's Cathedral Choir School, London. In 1890 he went into the city office of the Anglo-American (Standard) Oil Co. as a book-keeper. His earliest writings were fantasies. In 1902, under the pseudonym of Walter Ramal, he published his *Songs of Childhood*. In 1908 his distinction as a poet was recognized by a Civil List pension. His novel *Memoirs of a Midget* won for him the James Tait Black Memorial Prize, 1922. His recent collections of poetry include *Pleasures and Speculations* (1940); *Bells and Brass* (1941); *Collected Poems* (1942); *The Burning Glass* (1945); *The Traveller* (1946); *Inward Companion* (1950); *Winged Chariot* (1951). Died in 1956.

DURRELL, LAWRENCE

Born in 1912 in India. He left there for England at the age of twelve and was educated at St. Edmund's School, Canterbury. He has held Foreign Office posts in Athens, Cairo, Alexandria, and Belgrade. For a time he lived on the Greek island of Corfu. His publications include *A Private Country* (1943); *Prospero's Cell* (1943); *Cefalu* (1947); *On Seeming to Presume* (1948); *Sappho: A Play* (1950).

DYMENT, CLIFFORD

Born in 1914 at Alfreton in Derbyshire and educated at elementary and secondary schools. He has worked as a shop assistant, clerk and commercial traveller, and was a free-lance journalist for several years. Later he became a director of documentary films. He won the Atlantic Award in Literature in 1950. His verse publications include *Selected Poems* (1943) and *Poems, 1935-1948* (1949).

ELIOT, THOMAS STEARNS

Born in 1888 in St. Louis, Missouri, of a family with a strong religious tradition. His grandfather established the first Unitarian Church in St. Louis, and later founded Washington University. T.S. spent the first eighteen years of his life at St. Louis and was educated at Smith Academy of Washington. In 1906 he entered Harvard where he took his M.A. degree; then followed a year at the Sorbonne, after which he returned to Harvard to take his Ph.D. degree in Philosophy, studying logic, metaphysics, and Sanskrit. He went to Germany on a travel scholarship in the summer before the First World War; then to Merton College, Oxford to read philosophy. After his marriage in 1915, he earned his living by teaching at Highgate School, and later took a post in Lloyds Bank. It was from this time that he began to write seriously. His *Collected Poems, 1909-1925* were published in 1926 and included *Prufrock, The Waste Land*, and *The Hollow Men. Collected Poems, 1909-1935*, published in 1936, contained the first of his *Four Quartets*.

In 1922 he founded the literary review *The Criterion*, and soon after was appointed a Director of Faber and Faber, the publishers. He became a naturalized Englishman in 1927. Among the honours bestowed on him for his literary distinction are the Order of Merit, the Nobel Prize for Literature, and numerous honorary degrees.

He has had three verse plays performed: *Murder in the Cathedral, Family Reunion*, and *The Cocktail Party*.

FULLER, ROY

Born in 1912 at Faisworth, Lancs., and educated at Blackpool High School. He was admitted as a solicitor in 1934 and served with the Royal Navy from 1941 to 1946. He is at present Assistant Solicitor to the Woolwich Equitable Building Society. His interests are reading, classical music, watching soccer football, swimming, and writing poetry. He has published several books of poems, the most recent of which is *Epitaphs and Occasions* (1948). He has written two novels for young people and a book on Building Society Law.

GASCOYNE, DAVID

Born in 1916 and educated at Salisbury Cathedral Choir School and the Regent St. Polytechnic. He published his first book of poems at the age of sixteen, and his first novel at seventeen. In France, he fell under the influence of the French Surrealists, and translated many poems by Tzara, Éluard, and other writers in the movement. In 1935 he wrote a *Short Survey of Surrealism*. His later work shows little trace of this early influence, and he has written some religious verse. His latest publications are *Poems, 1937-1942* (1943) and *The Vagrant, and Other Poems* (1950).

GEE, KENNETH

Born in 1908 in Streatham and educated at Whitgift School, Croydon. His poems have appeared in many literary periodicals, and in *The Listener*. His published works are collections of short stories, and *Thirty-Two Poems* (1941). For the last twelve years he has been employed as a Local Government official in the Education Department. He finds relaxation, apart from reading and writing, in painting and music, and in exploring the coast of Sutherland, in north-west Scotland.

GRAVES, ROBERT

Born in 1895 and educated at Charterhouse and St. John's College, Oxford. He served in the First World War with the Royal Welch Fusiliers, and then returned to Oxford to read English Language and Literature. For a year he was Professor of English Literature in the University of Cairo. In 1909 he published his autobiography, *Goodbye to All That*. He took part in the Spanish Civil War on the side of the revolutionaries. He has lived mostly in Majorca. His verse publications include *Collected Poems, 1914-1947* (1948), but he is known to the general public more through his novels than his poetry: *I, Claudius* (1934); *Claudius the God* (1934); *Antigua Penny Puce* (1936); *Wife to Mr. Milton* (1943); *King Jesus* (1946); *The White Goddess* (1948); *Seven Days in New Crete* (1949); *The Isles of Unwisdom* (1950).

HAMILTON, SIR GEORGE ROSTREVOR

Born in 1888 in London and educated at Bradfield and Exeter College, Oxford. He entered the Inland Revenue Department in 1912, and subsequently held posts of increasing responsibility, until now he is the Presiding Special Commissioner of Income Tax. He was created a Knight in 1951. His recent verse publications include *The Sober War* (1940); *Apollyon* (1941); *Death in April* (1944); *Selected Poems and Epigrams* (1945); *Crazy Gaunt* (1946); *The Inner Room* (1947); *The Carved Stone* (1952).

JENNETT, SEÁN

Born on Nov. 12, 1912. His education was "incidental" and his career "erratic". He is a writer, typographer, publisher, printer, and lecturer. His interests are calligraphy, photography, drama, poetry, singing, art, and "taking things to pieces". His publications are *Always Adam* (1943), *The Cloth of Flesh* (1945), and *The Making of Books* (1951).

KING, FRANCIS

Born in 1923 in Adelboden, Switzerland, and educated at Shrewsbury School and Balliol College, Oxford. He has worked for the British Council in Florence and in Greece. In 1952 he was awarded the Somerset Maugham Award for his novel *The Dividing Stream*. His chief interests, apart from writing, are riding, music, and the theatre. He has written four novels, and a book of poems, *Rod of Incantation* (1952).

KIRKUP, JAMES

Has published *The Drowned Sailor, and Other Poems* (1947); *The Submerged Village, and Other Poems* (1951); *The*

Creation (1951); *The Correct Compassion, and Other Poems* (1952); and is frequently represented in *The Listener*. He prefers to be known through his poetry and considers that biographical details are extraneous and undesirable.

LEE, LAURIE

Born in 1914 in the Cotswold country. He spent some time in Spain before the Civil War. He published his first volume of verse, *The Sun My Monument*, in 1944, and his second, *The Bloom of Candles*, in 1947. A verse drama, *Peasant's Priest*, was performed at the Canterbury Festival. He has also had a verse play, *The Voyage of Magellan*, produced by the B.B.C.

LEWIS, CECIL DAY

Born in 1904 in Ireland and educated at Sherborne School and Wadham College, Oxford, where he was a contemporary of Auden, with whom he edited *Oxford Poetry*, 1927, and of Spender. He was a schoolmaster until 1935. During the Second World War he worked at the Ministry of Information, and since then he has devoted himself to writing, lecturing, and broadcasting, being now Professor of Poetry at Oxford University. In addition to his large output of poetry, which includes *Collected Poems, 1929-1936* (1937); *World Over All: Poems* (1943), and *Poems, 1943-1947* (1948), he has written novels, including some stories for children; he also writes detective novels under the pseudonym of Nicholas Blake.

LYON, LILIAN BOWES

Born in 1895 in Northumberland and educated privately. After the First World War she had eighteen months at Oxford, and worked later on farms in Northumberland. In 1940 she went to work and live among East End poor in Stepney and continued to do so throughout the bombing. She became seriously ill as a result and had both legs amputated, but in spite of constant pain, continued to write poetry until her death in June, 1949. Her *Collected Poems* were published in 1948.

MacNeice, Louis

Born in 1907 in Belfast, the son of the Bishop of Down, Connor, and Dromore, and educated at Marlborough and Merton College, Oxford. where he took a first in Classical Mods and Greats. He was appointed lecturer in Classics at Birmingham University in 1930, and lecturer in Greek at Bedford College, London University, in 1936. In that year he visited Spain and Iceland (the latter in company with Auden). He has lectured to university students in America, and held the post of Lecturer in Poetry at Cornell University for a short time in 1940. Since 1941 he has been a feature writer and producer for the B.B.C. His published works include collections of poetry, among them *Plant and Phantom* (1941); *Springboard: Poems, 1941-1944* (1944); *Holes in the Sky: Poems, 1944-1947* (1948); *Collected Poems, 1925-1948* (1949); *Ten Burnt Offerings* (1952); and several radio plays, including *The Dark Tower* (1947).

Masefield, John

Born in 1878, the son of a solicitor of Ledbury, Herefordshire, and educated at King's School, Warwick. At the age of thirteen he went to the *Conway* training ship in the Mersey. At fifteen and a half he was apprenticed aboard a windjammer and sailed round Cape Horn. He left the sea and stayed in New York for three years working his way through medical college, but abandoned this and took various jobs in bakeries, livery stables, saloons and a carpet factory. He began to write in 1897 and returned to England determined to be a writer. He originated the column " Miscellany " in the *Manchester Guardian*. His first collection of poems, *Salt-Water Ballads*, was published in 1902. Then came the vigorous, colloquial narrative poems: *The Everlasting Mercy* (1911); *The Widow in the Bye Street* (1912); *Dauber* (1913); and the play *The Tragedy of Nan* (1920). In the First World War he went with the Red Cross to France and Gallipoli. In 1922 he was given the honorary degrees of D.Litt.(Oxon.) and LL.D.(Aberdeen).

In 1930 he was appointed Poet Laureate, and in 1935 was awarded the Order of Merit. He has a considerable number of publications to his name, both in prose and verse, much of the latter being embodied in his *Poems* published in 1946.

MORLEY, AVERIL

Born on April 27, 1913, at Derby where her father, then in the Sherwood Foresters, was stationed. She is of Anglo-Irish stock and was educated at private schools. From 1937 to 1942 she was Assistant Secretary and later Research Assistant at the Edward Grey Institute, Oxford. In 1943 she joined the Scottish Land Army, and in 1944 was made Secretary and Research Assistant to the West Highland Survey, a post she held until 1948, when she married the well-known naturalist, F. Fraser Darling. She has written a number of scientific papers on bird behaviour. Her great interests, apart from poetry, are ornithology, natural history, and music. Her book of verse, *The House in the Forest, and Other Poems*, was published in 1946.

MUIR, EDWIN

Born in 1887 at Kirkwall in the Orkneys and educated at Kirkwall Burgh School until he was fourteen, when he went to Glasgow and became employed as a clerk by various commercial and shipbuilding firms. In the First World War he was rejected on health grounds. In 1919 he came to London as a free-lance journalist. Between 1921 and 1927 he lived in various European countries, supporting himself and his wife by writing. In collaboration with his wife, Willa Anderson, he made translations of the writings of Kafka, and was the means of introducing that writer to English readers. After 1934 he was co-editor of the *European Quarterly*, and was Director of the British Institute in Prague. He is now Warden of Newbattle Abbey College. His autobiography, *The Story and the Fable*, was published in 1940. His published poems include *Journeys and Places* (1937);

The Narrow Place (1943); *The Voyage, and Other Poems*
(1946); *The Labyrinth* (1948); *Collected Poems, 1921-1951*
(1952).

NICHOLSON, NORMAN

Born in 1914 in Millom, Cumberland—where he still lives
—and educated at local schools. He has a strong religious
sense, and edited the Penguin Anthology of Religious Verse.
He has lectured for the W.E.A. in the mining towns of
West Cumberland. He is specially interested in the revival
of verse drama, and his own play, *The Old Man of the
Mountains*, was chosen to open Martin Browne's season of
modern verse plays at the Mercury Theatre in 1945. It
has since been broadcast. He is now at work on a new verse
play about the prophet Hosea. His publications include
two collections of poems, *Five Rivers* (1944) and *Rock
Face* (1948); books on literary criticism, *H. G. Wells* (1950)
and *William Cowper* (1951); and in the County Books
Series, *Cumberland and Westmorland* (1949).

PALMER, HERBERT

Born in 1880 at Market Rasen, Lincs, and educated at
Woodhouse Grove School, Birmingham University and
Bonn University. From 1899 until the First World War he
was a schoolmaster, teaching French and German, but in
1921 he gave up teaching for literature and journalism. In
1932 he was granted a Civil List pension for his distinguished
work as a poet. He has published many volumes of poetry,
the most recent being *A Sword in the Desert* (1946) and *The
Old Knight* (1949).

PITTER, RUTH

Born in 1897 at Ilford in Essex. Her parents were teachers
in the East End and she was educated at the local elementary
school and then at Coborn School, Bow, London. She was
at the University when the First World War started, but
left and went to the War Office. Then she took a job with
an Arts and Crafts firm on the east coast and later opened a

similar business in Chelsea and made good. She has written verses since she was five. In 1937 she was awarded the Hawthornden Prize for the best imaginative work of the year with her collection of poems *Trophy in Arms*.

PLOMER, WILLIAM

Born in 1903 at Pietersburg, N. Transvaal, and educated at Rugby, after which he returned to Africa to engage in farming and trading. He has travelled widely, spending two years in Japan and later in Greece. In the Second World War he served at the Admiralty. He has written numerous novels, short stories, biographical works, and poetry, his verse publications including *Selected Poems* (1944) and *The Dorking Thigh* (1945).

PUDNEY, JOHN

Born in 1909 of farming parents and brought up to a business career which he abandoned for writing at the first opportunity. He was a B.B.C. writer and producer, and on the staff of the *News Chronicle* in the 1920's and 1930's. Several volumes of poetry resulted from his experiences in the R.A.F. during the Second World War—*Dispersal Point and Other Air Poems* (1943), *Ten Summers* (1944), and *Selected Poems* (1945); and he has written numerous short stories, several novels, and various books of travel, as well as the children's books, *Saturday Adventure* (1950), *Sunday Adventure* (1951), and *Monday Adventure* (1952).

RAINE, KATHLEEN

Born in 1908 in London and educated at Girton College where her chief interest was in Botany. She now lectures on poetry at Morley College and her published work in this field shows the influence of both her father, an English schoolmaster, and her Highland mother. The poet is constantly drawn to the remote Highlands and Scottish islands, where the primitive crofters, together with the birds, flowers, animals, and rocks, complete the full circle of life " where the primitive Celtic imagination fills the dark

spaces of the unconscious before birth and after death ". Miss
Raine also publishes highly valued reviews on literary
subjects and her critical work on Blake has been highly
praised. Her books of verse are *Stone and Flowers* (1943),
illustrated by Barbara Hepworth; *Living in Time* (1946);
The Pythoness, and Other Poems (1949); *The Year One* (1952).

READ, HERBERT

Born in 1893 in Yorkshire, the son of a farmer, and
educated at Crossley's School, Halifax, and Leeds University.
In the First World War he was awarded the D.S.O. and
the M.C. Then he entered the Civil Service and was for
ten years connected with the Victoria and Albert Museum.
He is best known as an authority on Art, and has published
many books on the subject. He has been Professor of Fine
Art in Edinburgh University, and has lectured on the same
subject in the Universities of Cambridge and Liverpool.
His verse publications include *Poems, 1914-1934* (1935);
Thirty-Five Poems (1940); *Collected Poems* (1946); *A World
Within a War* (1944).

REED, HENRY

Born in 1914 at Birmingham. After taking an M.A.
degree at Birmingham University where he was Charles
Grant Robertson Scholar, he took up free-lance journalism,
writing articles on literature and travel. Among other
work he did reviewing for the *New Statesman*. He was
called up in 1941, but released in 1942 when he went
to work at the Foreign Office. Since the war he has done
some broadcasting on books and films and has written
scripts for the radio. He has published one volume of
poems, *A Map of Verona* (1946), which contains a section
of war poems.

RIDLER, ANNE

Born in 1912 at Rugby where her father and uncle were
Housemasters at Rugby School. Her publications include
The Nine Bright Shiners (1943); *Cain* (1944); *The Shadow*

Factory (1946); *Henry Bly, and Other Plays* (1950); *The Golden Bird, and Other Poems* (1951). She also edited *A Little Book of Modern Verse* (1941) and the supplement to the new edition of Faber's *Book of Modern Verse*.

RODGERS, W. R.

Born in 1909 in Belfast. After taking his degree at Queen's University, Belfast, he studied for the Church, and from 1934 to 1946 he was minister of Loughall Presbyterian Church, Co. Armagh. Since 1946 he has been a script-writer and producer for the B.B.C. His first volume of verse, *Awake, and Other Poems*, was published in 1941, and his second, *Europa and the Bull, and Other Poems*, in 1952. In 1951 he was elected to the Irish Academy of Letters to fill the vacancy caused by the death of George Bernard Shaw.

ROSS, ALAN

Educated at Haileybury and Oxford (for which he played cricket and squash rackets). During the Second World War he was a naval officer in a destroyer. He is now Association Football correspondent to *The Observer*. His publications include *Poetry, 1945-50* (1952); *Time Was Away: A Notebook in Corsica* (1948) (with J. Minton); *The Forties* (1950); *The Gulf of Pleasure* (1951).

ROWSE, A. L.

Born in 1903 at St. Austell, Cornwall, and educated at the Elementary and County Schools at St. Austell, and at Christ Church, Oxford. He is now a Fellow of All Souls, Oxford. He is the editor of the *Teach Yourself History* Library. His recent publications include *Poems of Deliverance* (1946); *The End of an Epoch—Reflections on Contemporary History* (1947); *The England of Elizabeth* (1950); *The English Past* (1951).

SASSOON, SIEGFRIED

Born in 1886 in London. On his father's side he is descended from a wealthy Spanish-Jewish family; his mother is an artist. He was educated at Marlborough Grammar School and Clare College, Cambridge, but did not take his degree, being sent down for lack of interest in his studies. He devoted his time instead to poetry, hunting and tennis. In the First World War he went to France as a 2nd Lieutenant, served four and a half years, and won the M.C. He returned a pacifist and wrote anti-war poems. In 1928 he toured U.S.A. reading poetry and preaching pacificism. In 1928 he published *Memoirs of a Fox-Hunting Man*, which gained the Hawthornden Prize and the James Tait Black Memorial Prize. He has many publications to his name, his *Collected Poems* appearing in 1947.

SCOVELL, E. J.

No information available.

SITWELL, EDITH

Born in 1887 at Scarborough, the daughter of Sir George Reresby Sitwell and grand-daughter, on her mother's side, of the Earl of Londesborough. She was educated privately at home, and in 1916 began, with her two brothers, to edit an annual anthology *Wheels* in revolt against popular poetry of the time. In 1923 she recited a number of her poems, experiments in rhythm, to the accompaniment of music composed and played by William Walton (the composition known as *Façade*). She was awarded the Medal of the Royal Society of Literature in 1934 and has subsequently received various other honours for her outstanding gifts as a poet. She was given the honorary degree of D.Litt. of Leeds University in 1948, and of Durham and Oxford Universities in 1951, and in 1949 was made an Honorary Associate of the American Institute of Arts and Letters. Her recent publications include *A Poet's Notebook* (1943); *Green Song* (1944); *A Song of the Cold* (1945); *Fanfare for Elizabeth* (1946); *The Shadow of Cain* (1947); *A Notebook on William Shakespeare* (1948); *The Canticle of the Rose* (1949); *Poor Men's Music* (1950).

SNAITH, STANLEY

Born in 1903 and educated at Kendal and privately. He is at present Borough Librarian of Bethnal Green Public Library. From 1940 to 1942 he was Local Secretary to the Ministry of Information; then he served in H.M. Forces in Heavy Anti-Aircraft Batteries from 1942 to 1946. His recent publications include *Alpine Adventure* (1944); *Stormy Harvest* (1944); *The Inn of Night* (1946); *The Flowering Thorn* (1946) (with G. V. Vale); *The Naked Mountain* (1949); *The Common Festival* (1950); *The Mountain Challenge* (1952).

SPENDER, STEPHEN

Born in 1909 in London, of part German, part Jewish descent, and educated at University College School and University College, Oxford. When an undergraduate, he travelled considerably on the Continent, and went down from the university without his degree. Between 1929 and 1932 he lived several months of each year in Germany, his frequent companion being Isherwood. He was also a friend of Auden, having been, at Oxford, a contemporary of Auden, MacNeice, and Day Lewis. Like Auden and Lewis he professed himself a Communist when he left the University, but was attracted to it emotionally rather than rationally, though he remained strongly left-wing. During the Second World War he was a fireman in the London Auxiliary Fire Service. He has published many volumes of poetry, including *Poems for Spain* (1939); *Ruins and Visions* (1942); *Poems of Dedication* (1947); *The Edge of Being* (1949); and his autobiography, *World within World* (1950).

SUMMERS, HAL

Born in 1911 at Bradford in Yorkshire and educated at Jordanhill School, Glasgow, Fettes College, Edinburgh, and Trinity College, Oxford. He is a Civil Servant and has been connected with the Ministry of Health and later with the Ministry of Housing and Local Government.

His interests are mainly domestic, literary, and musical. He is also fond of walking in the country. His publications include *Smoke after Flame* (1944); *Hinterland* (1947); *Visions of Time* (1952).

THOMAS, DYLAN

Born in 1914 in Carmarthenshire and educated at Swansea Grammar School. He spent one year as a newspaper reporter. His first volume of poetry was published when he was only nineteen, and in 1938 he won the Oscar Blumenthal Prize offered by *Poetry* (*Chicago*). He was rejected for military service in the Second World War. He has worked for the B.B.C. His publications include *Eighteen Poems* (1934); *Twenty-five Poems* (1936); *The World I Breathe* (1939); *The Map of Love* (1939); *Portrait of the Artist as a Young Dog* (1940); *Deaths and Entrances* (1946); *Collected Poems, 1934-1952* (1952). Died in 1953.

TILLER, TERENCE

Born in 1916 in Cornwall and educated at Latymer School. He won a scholarship to Jesus College, Cambridge, in 1934, and was awarded the Chancellor's Gold Medal in 1936. Then he did two years' research in Medieval History, and later went as assistant lecturer in English to the University of Cairo. His publications are *Inward Animal* (1944) and *Unarm, Eros* (1948).

TODD, RUTHVEN

Born in 1914 and educated at Fettes College, Edinburgh. He was Sub-editor of *New Verse*, the leading poetry magazine of the 1930's. He has published novels and books of poems—*The Acreage of the Heart* (1944), *Planet in My Hand* (1946), and *Tracks in The Snow* (1946)—and is frequently represented in *The Listener* and other periodicals.

TREECE, HENRY

Born in 1912, of Welsh parentage. He has been a schoolmaster, artist's model, dance-band pianist, and was an

officer in the R.A.F. in the Second World War. His publications include *Black Seasons* (1945); *The Haunted Garden*
(1947); *The Dark Island* (1952).

WARNER, REX

Born in 1905. He spent his boyhood in Gloucestershire
where his father was a clergyman of the Church of England,
and was educated at St. George's, Harpenden, and Wadham
College, Oxford where he took a first class in Class. Hon.
Mods. He taught Classics and English for a time in England
and in Egypt. During the war he was schoolmaster in the
London area and afterwards, from 1945 to 1947, was
Director of the British Institute in Athens. His publications
include *Poems* (1937) and *Poems and Contradictions* (1945).
He has also written novels, essays, and translations from
Greek and Latin.

WATKINS, VERNON

Born in 1906 and educated at Repton and Magdalene
College, Cambridge. He served in the R.A.F. from 1941
to 1946. He was made a Fellow of the Royal Society of
Letters in 1951. He is now an official of Lloyds Bank.
His recreations are tennis, walking, swimming, rock-
climbing, and music. His publications include *The Ballad
of the Mari Lwyd, and Other Poems* (1941); *The Lamp and
the Veil* (1945); *The Lady with the Unicorn* (1948).

WELLESLEY, DOROTHY (Duchess of Wellington)

Her publications include *Poems* (1920); *Genesis* (1926);
Poems of Ten Years (1934); *Lost Planet, and Other Poems*
(1942); *Desert Wells* (1946); *Selected Poems* (1949); *Far
Have I Travelled* (1952). Died in 1956.

WHISTLER, LAURENCE

Born in 1912 and educated at Stowe School and Balliol
College, Oxford. He won the first King's Medal for
Poetry in 1934 with his *Four Walls*, and amongst subsequent
publications his *Collected Poems* appeared in 1949. In addition

to his work as a poet, he has recently taken up engraving on glass, and is regarded as one of the finest artists in this medium. Among the works he has produced is an engraved glass casket which, together with the poem engraved upon it, he designed for Queen Elizabeth, the Queen-Mother, as a present to the late King George VI shortly before his death.

WILLY, MARGARET

Born in 1919 in London and educated at Beckenham County School and Goldsmith's College (University of London). She worked in various publishing houses until the middle of the war and studied in her spare time between 1936 and 1940 for the University's Diploma in the Humanities (Eng. Lit.), in the course of which she was given the W. H. Hudson Prize for English Literature in 1938, and the Gilchrist Medal for Literature in 1940. From 1942 to 1946 she served in the Women's Land Army. In 1946 she was given an Atlantic Award in Literature and since then she has been a free-lance writer and has published reviews and poems. Her collected poems are *The Invisible Sun* (1946) and *Every Star a Tongue* (1951). She has also written literary essays. She is at present a part-time tutor in Literature for the British Council. Her interests are travel, people, gardening, and painting.

YOUNG, ANDREW

Born in 1885 at Elgin and educated at the Royal High School, Edinburgh, and Edinburgh University where he took his M.A. degree. He has been a Canon of Chichester Cathedral since 1948, and Vicar of Stonegate, Sussex since 1941. He was made an Hon. LL.D. of Edinburgh University in 1951, and is also a Fellow of the Royal Society of Letters. His publications include *A Prospect of Flowers* (1945); *A Retrospect of Flowers* (1950); *Collected Poems* (1950); and *Into Hades* (1952).

INDEX OF POETS

*(The bracketed numbers refer to the pages on which their poems
are to be found)*

INDEX OF FIRST LINES